Opening the Door to Enlightenment

Exploring Mystical Experiences and Expanded States of Consciousness

A Psychospiritual Guidebook

Aubrey Degnan, Ph.D.

Text Copyright © 2024 by Aubrey Degnan, Ph.D.
Illustration Copyright © 2024 by Mike Van Eps

Cover: Mike Van Eps
Editing and Layout: Vicki Anne Crane

First Edition February 2024
ISBN 979-8-9875778-3-7
eBook ISBN 979-8-9875778-4-4

Published by Miracle Publishing Group
www.miraclepublishinggroup.com

Opening the Door to Enlightenment is dedicated to
the commitment, fulfillment, and realization of
the highest states of consciousness abiding within all beings.

This guidebook is dedicated to you seeking to open to your essential nature
and courageously embark upon an ancient journey in modern times.

This guidebook is dedicated to the transformational work
of Men of Integrity (MOI), their rapidly growing community,
and friends around the globe.

Contents

Expressions of Gratitude

In life, there are those rare synchronistic moments when an introduction between friends leads to a full-blown immersion into a vibrant community of men and women dedicated to self-discovery, kindness, and service.

Let me tell you a story.

One day, Michael Van Eps (whom I have known for many years) tells me about a friend of his doing some very interesting work with men. That intuitive voice inside me says, "Oh, perhaps he would like a copy of my book? Would you give it to him?" Little did I know, that by hearing and following a moment of spontaneous guidance, my first book, *Luminous, the Psychology of Enlightenment*, would be so graciously received by Michael Tierno and would resonate with his path in guiding men and women. Within weeks, Michael Tierno, Michael Van Eps, and Yoni Havana appear at our doorstep on their way to a retreat. Within these precious moments, we clasp hands, gaze into the warm eyes of our new friends, and acknowledge the connection that is present in the space. These are powerful and special moments of meeting kindred souls.

Since then, many who have sought the guidance of Michael Tierno and Yoni Havana have come to work with me as follow-up to the more intensive retreat experiences. For the past year, I have heard their stories and witnessed their openings. These are men and women from many walks of life and a diversity of backgrounds who seek to live a life of harmony and love. In deeply listening to their stories, it becomes clear we need on-going inner work and a supportive community to solidify experiences of profound heart openings. Thus began our conversation and the creation of this psychospiritual guidebook, *Opening the Door to Enlightenment*.

Acknowledgements

As the founders of MOI, Michael Tierno and Yoni Havana have designed and implemented a visionary international program that is holistic, pragmatic, and spiritually inclusive. To date, their work has directly touched more than 100 people over a span of 8 years. Their work is currently expanding to include parents and significant others. Michael Tierno is a guide of expanded states of consciousness and offers retreats in the Sacred Valley of Peru as well as in California. Yoni Havana is a guide, activator, and podcast host, exploring the depths of consciousness. He offers individual retreat and sessions in Georgia and Florida. Their values of integrity, authenticity, kindness, gratitude, and accessing inner Divinity come to life in the experiences their work provides during retreats, individual work, and follow-up seminars.

Inspired leadership creates vision, spilling over into this guidebook through the beautifully interpreted illustrations of an accomplished visual effects and graphic designer Michael Van Eps. He is a member of The Academy of Motion Picture Arts and Sciences, receiving more than 70 film credits, and a member of the MOI training team.

I am grateful for their invaluable contributions to this guidebook. I thank each of you.

This guidebook contains numerous personal quotes from anonymous individuals who have directly experienced the impact of MOI. They share their expanded states of consciousness interwoven with psychological issues to be healed. Together, through their explorations, we are creating a map of human consciousness to better understand ourselves, to embrace challenges as opportunities, and to apply a healthy paradigm into our daily lives.

I thank each of you for so poignantly sharing your inner world in this guidebook. Truly, the richness and depth of your words bring to life the vision of MOI and its community.

In deep gratitude, I thank those who have supported the creation of this guidebook: Annie Crane, for her compassionate clarity, editorial feedback, boundless encouragement, and professional publishing knowledge making this book available. I thank Jess Van Eps for her editorial comments bringing inclusivity to this book. I thank my beloved husband, Tom, who enters the Emptiness daily and his careful conversations regarding these matters of the soul.

In profound gratitude, I thank Tarthang Tulku Rinpoche, my root guru and first Vajrayana spiritual teacher for the impact he has had on my life and subsequent work with others.

Chapter I

Psychological Aspects of the Inner Journey

Why Do We Come to this Inner Journey?

We enter this path sensing there is a much greater potential for our happiness, joy, and meaning in this life. We are growth-orientated, viewing the world as filled with opportunities. That which appears challenging is a lesson to be learned.

We enter this path perhaps as a seeker, not yet quite sure of what that means. However, the magnetic pull is present in our heart. There may be a *yearning*.

We enter this path as innocent children drawn to a familiar and yet unconscious yearning to return home. This deep yearning is part of our innocent childlike nature. This is our soul.

We enter this path perhaps due to synchronicity, unexpected hearing of a mysterious journey through a friend or family member. We feel the pull to explore as warriors entering new terrain. We are *curious*.

We enter this path of inner work because we are in *pain*—perhaps physical, relationship, emotional, financial, familial, loss of a cherished loved one, or in transition. Pain motivates us to change.

Three distinct internal movements are present in us: yearning, curiosity, and pain.

What Is this Inner Journey?

This is a journey of self-discovery; a journey of reconnection with our hearts, our inner voice, and with our loved ones.

Zen teachings call this "peeling the layers of the onion" with tears upon our cheeks. We empty our vessel. We release our pain, our past-based thinking, and our self-talk to reconnect with our deepest inner core. It is this core being that actualizes our potential into expanded states of consciousness.

This inner journey is a rebalancing, lessening our pain and strengthening our soul.

To undertake this journey, we need to heal our traumas and memories which caused us to abandon ourselves in order to survive. These actions became our defenses against remembering painful moments and also defending us against anticipated future pains. We closed down. This in turn leads to alienation, separation, and depression.

Now you must be a brave warrior, willing to discover whatever is inside you.

**Remember, whatever struggles you have gone through, you made it through.
You are here, now.**

What is Our Deeper Essential Nature?

There is a gradual process in how our soul moves into merging with the Oneness. Through peeling back the layers of ego and uncovering our inner child, we discover our soul. This process, in turn, allows us to taste a connection with all that is. Gradually, this last step evolves into a profound sense of resting, peacefully in a state of Oneness without any separation or identification. This is the rebalancing—less ego and more soul.

Our deeper essential nature is formless and in union with all that is. We come out from the one Source of creation (known by many as God, Allah, Heavenly Father, or Source). Deep inside is a flow of energy, formless and fluid in movement resting in front of your spine, from your perineum to your crown. The connection with God, Source, or Oneness is within this flow, simultaneously, uniquely you and all that is. There is a texture, perhaps a series of colors accompanied by sensations, pulsations, and warmth. This energetic flow gives rise to preverbal understandings or realizations about life and its purpose—our place in the universe.

From this total union without any separation, we gradually, mysteriously acquire a modicum of uniqueness. The moment there is any color, movement, energy that which has been without form begins to assume a semi-form. We are gradually becoming our unique soul. Focus inward towards your heart chakra in the center of your chest, a home of compassion and wisdom.

Layers Within the Human Psyche

There are layers within the human psyche. These layers intermingle throughout our daily life. We may act like our inner child when emotions flare up. We may keep "a stiff upper lip" when we need to put on a good face and go to work. When we yearn for peace and harmony, we are dipping into our deeper essential self. Thus, there are two primary reasons we do intense meditational retreats: to empty our pain and to taste peace.

In doing inner transformational work, there is a healing process helping us to gradually melt inauthentic facades into more positive and healthy versions of each layer.

- ✧ **Source/Divinity/Essence:** Our essential nature is pure light, love, and connection with all that is.
- ✧ **Soul:** A subtle energy that has tendencies carried from one life to another. We see this in infants as we comment, "What a wise soul you seem to be. "
- ✧ **Child:** Our innocent playful qualities.
- ✧ **Adult:** Our mature and responsible functioning in the world.
- ✧ **Role/Career:** The various roles we assume within a day, i.e. spouse, parent, career/work.

The illustration below shows one model for understanding these layers. There are many other models. However, this model expresses a philosophy akin to the layers of the onion—we peel back the layers to arrive at our core.

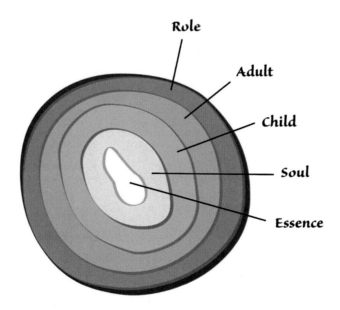

What Is Our Ego?

Ego obscures the clarity and love that abides in our essential nature.

Ego refers to our conditioned self. This conditioned self has a role in society, helping us function and providing cognitive decision-making. This conditioned self has both unhealthy habits and positive qualities. There are two sides of one coin.

This conditioning process begins when we are in our mother's womb. We hear sounds. The birthing experience has a powerful impact upon our conditioning. Was it an easy birth or were there unforeseen events that produced trauma like low oxygen levels? Many people are aware of early childhood traumas or negative imprinting that is verbal and non-verbal.

As adults, we are more familiar with "triggers." We recognize our buttons are being pushed as we react with strong emotion and a sense of tension. This tells us we have not **yet** healed an early childhood scene.

Transformation of Negative Ego Habits

For example, if there has been physical or emotional abuse you experienced or witnessed as a child, there is a tendency to repeat these situations as an adult. Here, one needs to heal the scene of origin, rewrite the script, and let it go. Each of these is a process that takes some time. However, we can rewrite the script once we have relived the original scene in some detail under the work with a guide.

In doing inner work, the conditioned ego naturally transforms from negative emotions into more positive, healthy emotions.

For example: **Anger transforms into a quality of serenity.**

The conditioned ego in this case was imposing its conviction of what is perfect onto itself and others. This ego has a lot of "should(s)" and judgments. This ego often feels not good enough or bad. In the process of healing, the conditioned ego lessens its grip and transforms into an acceptance of what is. Here, the perception shifts into observing what is as its own perfection. This is the natural transformation.

To give a second example: **Fear and doubt transform into courage.**

Here, the haunting perception of underlying fear of whatever faces us in our current life causes inner conflict. There is a continual "yes" and "no" to each and every thought we have. This ego has a lot of "but(s)" in its sentences. Here, transformation is helped by using the word "and" in place of "but."

"I want to _____, but I'm scared." This language paralyzes the person. There is no action taken because of telling oneself, "I am scared." Being scared becomes the controlling emotion. However, if you just change the word "but" to "and," there is an entirely different response: "I want to _____, and I am scared." Okay, got it, I'm scared. So, exhale the fear, and try something new: DO IT! Whatever you are scared about, give it a try. Perhaps the new behavior or decision will actually bring about an excitement!

Many of the people who experience the work of Men of Integrity (MOI) want deeper friendship where they can open and share what is really happening on the inside. I often hear, "I want to be more vulnerable and honest, but I'm afraid to. Maybe no one will really listen or care." Change the sentence to, "I want to be more vulnerable and honest, and I'm afraid to." That new statement is honest, vulnerable, and expressing feelings, including the emotion of fear. Yet, again, fear no longer stops the action. Rather, the fear, along with other desires for meaningful friendship, co-exists.

This frees the ego from conflict, wherein the world pressures us to be either this or that. This is duality. There is no inclusiveness. Transformation of this fear changes into courage. This courage even welcomes opportunities for growth. Note the physiological similarities between fear and excitement. The difference is in the perception. This is quite liberating! Previously, there had been a paralysis due to fear. Now, the world opens to new possibilities.

How Is Ego Conditioned?

Our ego is an aspect of our psyche that has developed habits over many years. These habits lock us into patterns of behavior that often alienate us, causing unhappiness and stress.

The process of conditioning begins when we are in the womb hearing sounds, feeling the nervous system of our mother soften or constrict. The events of our birth and the first few hours of life carry another profound impact upon our worldview. Our childhood is filled with do(s) and don't(s), most of which were beyond our control.

We watch our parents and model their behavior. We hear their beliefs and adopt similar views. However, we can also rebel against these behaviors and beliefs and the inner pendulum swings to a counter position. In both examples, we are a victim of subtle rules and beliefs about reality adopted through a conditioning process—"victim" because these behaviors and beliefs are not coming from a deeper place inside us that has freedom of choice. We become trapped in limiting core beliefs and reactive behaviors.

Limiting Core Beliefs and Their Transformation

Limiting core beliefs are learned as we observe our parents' behavior, tonality, and emotions. We assume what they are showing us is true about life. We mimic their behaviors. We further assume we must do as they do in order to survive. This is a judgment, not a reality. Beliefs are not reality. However, we make them into reality by believing in them. Feeling not good enough no matter how hard you try is a limiting core belief.

Slowing It Down: Step I

During an individual intensive eight-hour session, a client discovers a limiting core belief:

> *"I just see how much goodness there is in my life and that I like discount it. There's a part of me that feels like things shouldn't be good or great. It's like they shouldn't be that way or I don't deserve them. Other people deserve to be happy, but not me."*

At this point as the guide, I slow down the words being said by suggesting we unpack these phrases. Initially, the client states, "How much goodness there is in my life." This is the deeper voice of her essential nature making a true statement about the qualities in her life. This positive and healthy attitude comes from a deeper, self-compassionate inner voice: our soul.

Then, rapidly, without skipping a nanosecond, along comes her negating, demeaning, and conditioned ego countering the compassionate voice. Here is the beginning of the limiting core belief firmly admonishing the audacity of the soul to even speak.

"Remember," states the conditioned ego, "we were taught over and over again that we don't deserve, that we are not good enough, and that we are less than." The voice of her soul is countered verbally, behaviorally, and energetically saying, "I don't deserve." This voice comes from her conditioned ego having internalized messages such as, "No, that's not for you. That's for so-and-so."

Much of traditional therapy gets stuck at this point. It is the trap of the "story" leading to a never-ending litany of re-examination of all the times we were hurt, demeaned, and judged. This is the old school of "healing," the trap of the story.

Slowing It Down: Step II

Conversely, I suggest we continue to slow down the process. We are at a juncture: you can go the **old way** or you can go a **new way.**

Without countering the undeserving voice, without negating this voice, I suggest the client restate, *"How much goodness there is in my life,"* several times. Each time, she needs to pay careful attention. How does it feel to be saying her own words? There is a progressive embodying of awareness of **sensations** that accompany the experience. Then I ask, "Where do you feel goodness? Now rest there for a few moments and let that goodness feeling go even deeper." The client next initiates, *"I do deserve goodness. I am goodness!"*

After this sequence, I ask her, "How do you feel now?" This brings even greater awareness to a deeper discovery of what "goodness" feels like in the body, in the senses, and in the perception. I encourage her to look at the room and note the changes in perception. "How does this room look now as compared to when you first came in?"

There are several dynamics at play here. The shift in perception comes with a taste of freedom, a deep relief, a weight lifted from her shoulders. This taste is a hint of expanded states of consciousness wherein we feel more space and more present. This taste impacts our significant relationships, allowing us to disentangle from the web of anticipated triggers. Where previously there is an anticipation or projection of something going wrong, now there is less or no anticipation of this limiting core belief. We are freer and less reactive.

Slowing It Down: Step III

In follow-up individual sessions with a client who has tasted the healing of a limiting core belief, I take the next step: Rewrite the script.

Encouraged by settling into the sensations that come with feeling goodness and the freedom it brings from judging everything in life, oneself and others, and all events, there remains one final piece. For this step, they need an extra boost of strength: **the willingness to let go of being stuck in the mud and mire of their own suffering. Are you willing to go further?**

Are you ready to step into a life where the old story becomes a passing thought? You recognize the pattern as it arises. In the first nanosecond of the thought forming, you say, "I have a choice." Breathe. Feel the goodness inside. Remind yourself that you truly are creating a new paradigm for the rest of your life. This implies your perception, your attitudes, your emotions, and lastly your external actions and words move in a new direction.

You have removed the shackles of childhood conditioning and replaced it with self-determination. With greater freedom and self-realization, we are more connected to others through our hearts. We feel our environment more deeply, seeing its exquisite beauty. When you feel goodness, you treat others with goodness. As they say, "random acts of kindness." This shift in perception brings a new life!

Let us take another example, rewriting the script as parents of young children. In a seemingly normal interaction, a parent tells their child a toy belongs to their playmate. *"No, give that back to Tommy. It's his toy,* not *yours."* The parent's voice carries a tone of admonition. The child is being told *"No, that's not for you. That's for Tommy."* This carries a message that the child is less important than their friend, Tommy. Tommy gets the toy. The deeper dynamic here is the child does not deserve to be happy. This becomes a limiting core belief, *"I don't deserve to be happy."*

From the perspective of the parent, they think they are teaching boundaries and respect. While true in one aspect, there is a subtle **omission of love**. In working with a client who uncovers this scene from their childhood, or in working with a parent of young children, this moment is ripe for rewriting the script.

In the new script, as the parent gives the toy back to Tommy, they simply hand their child another toy saying, *"This is your special toy. I love you. Enjoy!"* Here, the emphasis shifts from the take away to being given something special. **This is love.** We overlook the importance of love. We leave it out. We need to bring it in. More.

Another example of the rewriting of the script is the groundbreaking work of Neuro-linguistic Programming, popularized by Tony Robbins. In the limiting core belief of fear, "I can't do it," "it" becomes an endless story of being stuck and paralyzed into non-action. Tony suggests changing the word "can't" to "won't," thereby invoking the person's anger or fire. By upping their energy level into a more forceful tone, the word next transforms into "must." Tony's motto becomes, "If I can't, I must!"

We walked over 40 feet of hot coals just to prove we could. We climbed telephone poles just to prove we could. We tested our mind's ability to focus on the positive while we physically performed daring acts just to prove we could. Today, you sit in cold plunges just to prove you can.

This is rewriting the script.

The Enneagram

A long, long time ago, the early roots of humanity were said to have lived in the mountains and valleys of the Tigress and Euphrates Rivers, deep in what today is the Middle East. This land was later the home of the hidden Sufi wise men known as the Sarmouni. It is said that Jesus, in his teenage years, traveled to parts unknown to study with the Sarmouni. It is further said that Gurdjieff studied with the Sarmouni. What we know for sure is that Oscar Ichazo studied with the Sarmouni and, in turn, Dr. Claudio Naranjo received these teachings. Today, this lineage is presented as the Enneagram of Personality.

These esoteric teachings are intended to be passed from teacher to disciple in direct relationship to the ego fixation or needs of the student. Unfortunately today, the popularization through the internet has diminished the true intent which is self-discovery through observation, not through pablum spoon-fed tests.

However, be that as it may, here is a taste of the original teachings passed to us through Dr. Claudio Naranjo, a Chilean psychiatrist who introduced this profound system in 1970 to his students in Berkeley. Claudio states, "Fixations are delusions at the heart of our personality. Behavior is compulsive and can no longer be spontaneous or creative."

While limiting core beliefs can be formed within a single event during childhood, our conditioned ego is formed over a period of time. This larger construct becomes a pattern with numerous characteristics that are both self-defeating and self-liberating. This is the purpose of the study of the Enneagram and its patterns.

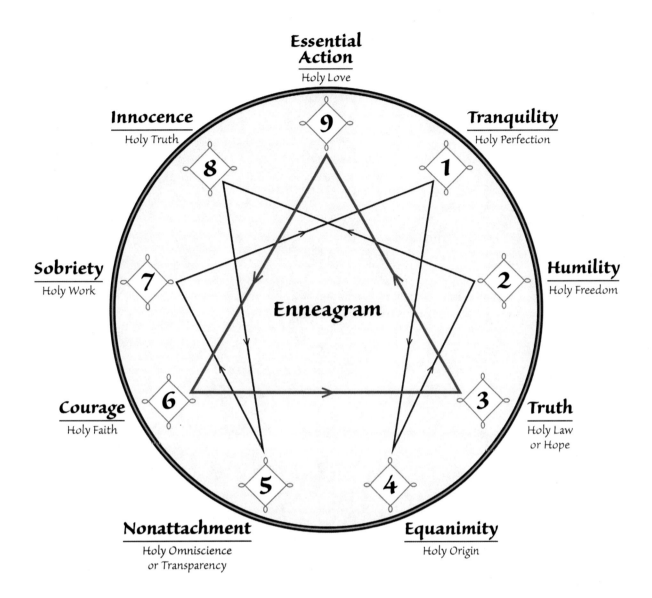

In keeping with the purity of Claudio's teaching transmission and intent, I will only briefly introduce these ideas, allowing one's own self-discovery to occur through study rather than cognitive ideas or internet tests.

This system is quite intricate and designed to be studied to identify one's primary ego fixation or point on the Enneagram. There are nine personality types, three corresponding body types, and three basic instincts. Each primary personality type has two wings and two inner flows.

Yet, to be simple in our first approach to understanding the pattern of your conditioned ego, it is best to focus upon:

- ✦ What is my primary negative passion?
- ✦ What is the main characteristic of my conditioned ego?

Fixation Point	Passion	Main Characteristic	Rationalization
#1 Ego Perfect	Anger	Perfectionism	"I am righteous."
#2 Ego Flat	Pride	Wet/Flattery	"I am helpful."
#3 Ego Vanity	Lying	Ego Go	"I am successful."
#4 Ego Melon	Envy	Melancholy	"I am correct."
#5 Ego Avoidance	Attachment	Withdrawal	"I know."
#6 Ego Fear	Fear	Spiritual Stuttering	"I am loyal."
#7 Ego OK	Gluttony	Charlatanism	"I am okay."
#8 Ego Venge	Lust/Excess	Vengeful	"I can do."
#9 Ego Indolence	Indolence	Laziness to Self	"I am comfortable."

Here are both the powerful passions (pseudo feelings) of each fixation point and their corresponding transformational virtue (quality of energy i.e. a true feeling):

Fixation Point	Passion	Virtue
#1 Ego Perfect	Anger	Serenity
#2 Ego Flat	Pride	Humility
#3 Ego Vanity	Lying	Truthfulness
#4 Ego Melon	Envy	Equanimity
#5 Ego Avoidance	Attachment	Detachment
#6 Ego Fear	Fear	Courage
#7 Ego OK	Gluttony	Sobriety
#8 Ego Venge	Lust/Excess	Innocence
#9 Ego Indolence	Indolence	Action

These stuck aspects of ego can also be transformed into virtues. The transformation is not through effort to become a certain positive way, rather the transformation occurs naturally as the less healthy aspects of ego are slowly erased through intentional inner work.

Below are two examples of the psychodynamics within Fixation **#1** Ego Perfect (Anger/Serenity) and Fixation **#6** Ego Fear (Fear/Courage).

Ego Perfect

Here, our thoughts constantly justify why our position is "correct." Our language includes the word "should" on a regular basis. Our self-talk creates a filter upon how we perceive our reality and those around us. Somehow, we never quite measure up… we are never good enough. Or someone else is bad and I am good. We project our ego view of what is "perfect" onto the world. Thus, we never measure up to this critical and judgmental way of behaving. We impose this projection of standards onto ourselves and those around us in a never-ending spiral of demands and unmet standards. It is a lose/lose game.

If we are raised in a family where there is verbal abuse, tension, fighting, and arguing, we often repeat these behaviors in our own relationships. That modeling leads to anger, frustration, and continual irritation.

Ego Fear or Cosmic Stutterer

If one parent is fearful as a general attitude about life, often warning us of imminent dangers approaching, we, too, live within a fear-based life as adults.

If we live in fear, we have self-talk that is filled with doubt. We express this as conflict. There is the internal "yes voice" and the internal "no voice." Between the yes and the no, we experience paralysis, taking a course of no action. We are stuck in doubt.

For Ego Perfect, the roots of this fixation lay in a seemingly simple statement: "I'm okay." However, this smile, this almost pleasing façade of "I'm okay" really is far from the serenity it seeks. To transform, the smile must soften and feel itself.

For Ego Fear, the roots of this fixation lay in a self-paralysis—a deadness to one's personal and most deep essential needs. This fixation is called "cosmic stutterer" because the roots of self- doubt continue all the way to Enlightenment. Tenacious roots. Thus, to heal and transform, the person needs to take action for their own benefit as distinct from action for the benefit of others.

There is a direct correlation between reducing the vice grip of ego and accessing our essential nature.

For our spiritual life to grow strong and sustain more open states of consciousness with their concurrent positive emotional states, our ego needs to reduce its grip on our concept of self. People erroneously think that their conditioned self is their true self. After all, they have lived with this ego self for many years and it is familiar.

When people first hear phrases such as "let go of your ego," it is intimidating. In fact, what is being said is that you are more than your conditioned self. **You have greater potential in this life.**

There is a tradeoff: in exchange for letting go of this conditioned ego, how you were raised and the traumatic events you have experienced, you gain access to a more fulfilling and healthy life.

You feel greater connection with community in place of prior alienation. You reconnect with deeper hopes and dreams that, somehow along the way, were lost in the drive for success, money, and power. You left behind your ability to "be" and lived in a world of "doing." Not that there is anything awry in doing, achieving goals while living in this physical body. It's just that we limit ourselves by self-imposing goals that, once achieved, feel empty.

What Are the Steps on this Psychological Journey?

While this journey is far from linear, paradoxically, there is a fairly predictable course of events to bring about our healing.

Initially, we become aware: "I am anxious." "I feel stressed and uncomfortable." "I need to change something in my life." Just the act of hearing oneself, of acknowledging something is off here inside me, is an important step on this journey.

Anxiety sits like a lid on a pressure-cooker. Anxiety is on the surface, trying desperately to keep down what is trying to come up into our consciousness. The paradox is that when life seems to be going well, our anxiety mounts. Why? Because our inner voice that has repressed all these emotions and the impact of trauma is calling out to be heard. We are internally ready to deal with repressed material. We are stronger. Maybe we are living in a situation that has more support and understanding. We sense we can safely be heard.

In working with a guide, a therapist, a coach, we identify an emotion or issue causing the greatest discomfort. We pattern-trace our emotions and our somatic responses to a specific moment(s) in early childhood. We relive these formative scenes with careful details: who was present, who was absent, and what happened from the perspective of our inner child.

Here, the child was alone, in a sense a victim of the situation. This is where the inner child shuts down and puts up a defensive wall. Part of our self is left behind while externally we continue to grow into adults.

This is the moment where we give up and abandon our childlike nature. Sometimes, we stop feeling. Sometimes, we shut down even hearing our inner voice because, in fact, we were told to not speak up. Thank goodness there is a knowingness or wisdom in this inner child that, later in life, we can return to and hear and respect.

These kinds of events may be singular or may have repeated many times during our youth. If these events begin in utero, at birth, or up to two or three, it impacts our sense of self-preservation. If these events occur between five and nine, we struggle more with social concerns as an adult. If these events come as our body approaches adolescence, we place more priority onto our sexuality.

The goal of health is to have these three basic instincts in a state of harmony and balance. In the Sufi tradition of the Enneagram, these concerns are identified as self-preservation, social, and sexual. These three are in a state of imbalance until inner work is done to realign them.

There are traumas in our teenage and young adult years that again trigger unresolved incidents. These often show themselves through anxiety and the dis-eases that present as physical symptoms such as high blood pressure, heart irregularities, headaches, sexual issues, and anxiety.

To truly empty our vessel, we need to bring all the old and the current issues to consciousness. We can write them. We can paint them. Through a guided visualization with our eyes closed, we can relive them with an intention to heal. This implies that whatever conversation did not occur in the original scene can now be voiced. We can speak our unsaid(s) until the souls of the other people present actually acknowledge being spoken to.

What does this imply? This implies that somewhere and somehow souls can hear us. It implies that there are no secrets in the collective greater awareness of the Universe.

On the physical plane, we speak out loud to the people in the scene we are healing. For example, if we were a victim of an event such as verbal or physical abuse or emotional neglect, we tell the adult who was present how we feel about this situation. In our mind's eye, we look at the expression of the person whom we are addressing. Are they hearing you? Is their face stoic? Then, we speak again until their expression appears to soften, perhaps even to show regret or sorrow.

In our mind's eye, we perceive these expressions. Is this our projection? Or is this truly seeing a change in the soul in front of us? We may never exactly cognitively understand this. What we do know is that this inner moment impacts our psyche and the behavior of the person we are addressing. The external behavior of this person changes in our current life.

Yes, this may sound woo-woo. However, after decades of doing this approach to healing, we have seen these phenomena to be accurate.

This psychospiritual healing moves through several stages:

- ✧ Intellectually, we identify an anxiety.

- ✧ Emotionally, we feel stress.

- ✧ Somatically, we feel constriction in a specific part of our body.

- ✧ Energetically, we loosen and pull out the threads or sinews of anguish.

- ✧ Spiritually, we speak to the soul of the other.

- ✧ Physically, we open our eyes to carefully note, "How do I perceive this room right Here and Now?"

At this point, people often report:

"The room seems more spacious."
"It is more bright."
"The colors are more alive."

Here, the guide or therapist suggests the use of "I" to affirm and connect fully with this change of perception:

"I am more spacious."
"I am more bright."
"I am more alive."

These qualities of spacious, bright, and alive are accurate descriptions of an expanded consciousness.

This also implies that through the healing process of reliving, completing the conversation of the past, and returning to the Here and Now, we have moved from a place of pain to a space of expansion. This process is a meticulous cleansing that results in an integrated expansion of conscious into one's daily life.

Chapter II

Spiritual Aspects of the Inner Journey

Transpersonal Psychology emerged as a new philosophy in Western psychology when the Beatles brought music and meditation together, and Timothy Leary and Richard Alpert brought Enlightenment through LSD into our culture. "Turn on, tune in, and drop out." Turn on with psychedelics. Tune into one's essential nature and into the universal harmony. And drop out of this crazy social world.

"God is in the daisy." Flower children brought playful hope to a capitalistic generation. The cutting edge of Eastern wisdoms merged into the institutions and universities of the West. Facilitators leading workshops on military bases called themselves "change agents." However, this initial wave of pursuit of expanded consciousness receded. Research, the FDA, and the collective traditional social structure pushed back, hanging onto the more conservative views.

There is a parallel here between the reactions of society and the psychological reactions of an individual. There was a social breakthrough and then a receding. People have breakthrough experiences and then a receding. Today, on a social level, there is greater momentum towards Enlightenment and expanding states of consciousness. There is another wave building socially and internally.

This is an opportunity to change your focus from a past-based reality into a forward-looking excitement about life's potentials. Treat everything as a challenge. Cultivating a growth mindset implies enjoying life, learning new ways of being, and making efforts to explore your own potential. This is a creative endeavor where you get to be in the driver's seat.

In 1960, two Harvard University professors, Timothy Leary and Richard Alpert, conducted the groundbreaking Harvard Psilocybin Project. [1] This led the way to a careful Western approach to the consciousness of the human experience before and after death, as well as in altered states of consciousness including the loss of ego, time, and space. Their thesis was that the trajectory of these kinds of peak experiences could be mapped. And secondly, that students of this inner journey would be helped by having a road map, a familiarity with the transitions, emotions, visualizations, and power to prepare them for a more personal experience.

Mystical states tend to follow a trajectory, initially as a gentle taste or a powerful crescendo of energy. They peak only to gradually lessen into the more familiar terrain of ego. A less intense back and forth rhythm follows between breakthrough and ego.

For example, in the context of a retreat, a person may realize an Enlightened state, filled with profound connection to the Divine (this can last for days), then a gradual return to their more usual sense of self happens. However, the taste of Enlightenment never leaves.

The work is to sustain these states.

To sustain these breakthroughs of light, energy, kindness, and personal commitment to change takes support of community, personal diligence, and a good taste of one's own potential happiness.

To live in a state where perceptions are free from conditioning allows our innate clear mind to see the "Is-ness" without judgment. There are two steps here. First, the visual field becomes more pristine. Literally our physical vision perceives colors and forms whereas before we were not aware of the colors and did not pay attention to the forms. We might say, "Gosh, I just did not notice the flowers on the table." The lack of clarity is a reflection of a clouded perception, clouded by a busy mind and not being present. The second step is to just see what is before you with awareness. Here, you are more peaceful and present. There is no internal self-talk or story that leads to judgment. These momentary breakthroughs into being present and seeing what actually IS before us lead us into a more fulfilling life.

Each opening of the mind and heart brings a freedom, clarity, kindness, peace, and purpose that enhances our wellbeing and spills over into our relationships with our self, others, and our environment.

To live without inner commentary allows our deepest potential to speak and be heard. We connect first with ourselves. Through hearing ourselves, our life purpose becomes clearer. We bring that deep inner longing, our voice, into our daily lives. Yearnings become reality. We can create the life we want with its fullness, vitality, and love.

Our initial intent is to heal from trauma, from early childhood or prenatal conditioning, tangled interpersonal relationships, ancestral wounds, or a natural transition as we age. The surface motivation in our awareness is to reduce pain. Some may not be aware that pain is an underlying cause of addiction or self-soothing behavior. They simply want to feel better. This suffering brings enough discomfort that we realize, "I am hurting and want to do something about it." We approach with a conscious intent to change something. Motivation to heal is the beginning.

Healing may be physical. It may be emotional. It may be karmic residues from other times. Through reliving the freeze-frame mental images of struggle, we speak our unsaid words. Be a courageous warrior! This releases anger, tears, and fear. We need to get these emotions out of our bodies, relieving the muscular and neurological constriction of "body memories."

Body memories are released through breath practices in both Eastern and Western traditions. In the Western psychological approach, the sound "HA" relieves deep constrictions in the abdomen. In the Eastern spiritual approach, the holding of the breath and then rapid exhale also stimulates moving energy out of the belly. These powerful releases move the energy or Qi (chi) in our meridians. Then when we open our eyes, we are more present. This is the moment to claim our awareness by using "I" statements. "I am more bright." This is a baby step to a shift in consciousness where the client embodies the sensation of energy moving inside as well as third eye vision of rivulets of light flowing in the body.

With hearing one's own words, there is an affirmation that settles deep inside bringing a sense of security and gratitude.

In time, these few minutes of tasting this shift of perception and its accompanying sense of freedom grows into the spiritual liberation of Enlightenment. Freedom comes through "hearing." In the same vein that our visual perception transforms into clarity, our hearing transforms into greater awareness of sounds around us as well as hearing on a deeper level what is being said to us verbally. We resonate with hearing drums and symphonies. Literally, our hearing becomes more acute.

Longer retreats intensify breakthroughs, offering a quality of support that our biological family may not offer. In this setting, we are deeply heard and cared for by like-minded participants. We are going through this process together as a community. Follow-up, both in group settings and individual sessions, support integration back into our daily life. This part of the process is essential for firmly developing new patterns of thinking.

We become more skilled in letting go of habitual thought patterns. We now understand why we need silence in our minds. Our hearts feel more open. To support these tender changes, follow-up is so important.

With a modicum of stillness between our thoughts, we become more connected with our environment and others. In time, inner stillness, this dropping into the Here and Now, becomes a portal to expansion of consciousness. We begin to actualize our potential.

The spiritual journey is ancient—billions of years of memories stored in each cell. Each person's path is unique. The timing is individual. The steps are not linear. Purification and inner washing is part of the journey.

Mapping the Crescendo of Peak Experiences

Many Eastern and Western esoteric traditions produce mystical experiences in their students. **These fleeting moments vary in intensity and duration.**

Experiences

However, this journey is greater than a handful of experiences. This journey, in its fullness, aspires to sustain mystical experiences while walking through our daily lives. We need a personal map.

Perhaps the most complete mapping of consciousness comes to us through the Hindu and Buddhist cultures. Eastern psychology offers us a long history of detailed observation of the range of human consciousness along with an enormous literature of practical methods for controlling and changing that consciousness.

We come to retreats and individual sessions with an agenda prepared by our conditioned ego-self. It is this aspect of ego that writes, "What are my goals?" At best, we come willing to be in the Here and Now, open to what arises. Openness implies a readiness, a softening of the ego to explore our own Unknown. The journey continues as we stand on the edge of that which we do not *yet* understand. Perhaps a better question would be, "What are my aspirations?"

The deeper voice in you that contemplates, "What are my aspirations?" is entertaining new terrain. As of yet, there is no true Awareness or understanding as to the depth of the inquiry. And yet, once in a retreat or intensive session at the peak of the crescendo, the high point of a line graph, there are fleeting moments of insights, sounds, images, or memories, far beyond the familiar concept of space/time that rapidly come and go. The initial moment arises unexpectedly, gaining momentum followed by a gradual descent, returning to a more familiar state. Yet we are changed as we re-enter our daily life.

There may be hints of brilliant light or powerful electric torrents entering the top of our head, streaming throughout our nervous system. There may be the Void—a vast, spacious Emptiness. There may be wave upon wave of vibrating particles of universal energies. There may be a voice or presence guiding you.

We feel profound connection with all that is. Releasing fear and control, we leave behind our smaller concept of self. We taste a delicious Oneness Consciousness. This expanded awareness has quite specific qualities, e.g., clear, vast, open, and wise. On an emotional level, we feel peace, calm, freedom, kindness, patience, gratitude, and bliss.

Visually, we may perceive tiny particles of squiggly light moving before us. In the West we call this Brownian Movement, while in the East it is called the "thigles." It is a viewing of particles on a microscopic level that reveals there is no solidity to form. There may be waves of color and movement. There may be a shimmering quality, much like looking at a black road that shimmers with reflective light.

Resting in this state of expanded Awareness allows us to *be*. The *do*er of ego is cast aside. We feel equanimity and acceptance. Our very demeanor emanates love. We perceive beauty. Our creativity unfolds. The sculpture below, "Woman," exquisitely demonstrates innate creativity arising as we open. A member of the MOI community created this piece.

"Woman"

These are experiences of our deepest nature, our natural mind, our essential nature. Ego has released us and the doors to perception are wide open, beyond words and concepts.

Whether the journey be through external discovery—such as the James Webb Space Telescope breaking asunder man's concepts of the galaxy or through internal discovery contemplating, tasting, Enlightened states of consciousness—we are expanding! Expanding inward and outward at a rapid pace at this point in our existence.

How can we best nurture these precious tastes of the totality of Oneness? And to what end?

There are two distinct reasons:

✧ First, to improve the quality of our daily lives, bringing in greater harmony, meaning, clarity, productivity, and longevity.

✧ Second, to prepare us for our physical passing into the Bardo of Death with an awareness guiding us into the light and into peace.

The purpose of a guide is to record our experiences, to encourage us to remain in these peak moments just a few minutes longer, and to remind us of the importance of the inner work we have done. Guides help us have continuity as we return to our daily lives.

Recognizing the meaning of peak moments is known as the generation stage—to be ultimately cultivated and nurtured into a fruition that remains with us during our lifetime.

Esoteric traditions call us householders, as distinct from monks or nuns. We live in the material world, in a society that values competition, image, and material possessions. Once the money is made, the babies are raised, or we return from a war, our values may shift into a more introverted focus. We are looking for a deeper purpose or meaning to life.

This shift provides a fertile backdrop for the inner journey including **1)** living a full life, and **2)** dying in peace with a sense of completion. This has been a good life. I am prepared for the next journey. I have tasted the Void, the Emptiness, and the love. I recognize the brilliance of the light. I have a modicum of ability to still my mind. I am prepared.

Questions about our spiritual purpose come to the fore. These questions combined with inner work lead to a more contemplative (or more yin) aspect of the human psyche.

It is the feminine aspect of our human psyche that yields and welcomes. The powerful force of the masculine rushes through every cell. These two aspects co-mingle into ecstatic states of union sexually as humans and cosmically as souls. It is a progression that is non-linear, universal yet individual. These are the higher tantric practices of cosmic union.

Transitional States of Consciousness: The Six Bardos

Why are these called "transitional states"? Because within a single day, we move through different states of consciousness without really recognizing these shifts, let alone being able to guide them ourselves.

Consciousness is not the content of a thought. Rather, consciousness is more an awareness, a sensing without words. Before a thought enters our mind, we have moments that are still. This is awareness. We may hear sounds and feel sensations without putting labels onto the experience.

To lead a healthy life, we need balance between mental activities and absence of mental activity. We need breaks, such as daydreaming where we gaze out the window, or stretch and walk.

Then, we return to focus upon a task at hand. Here, our brain activity moves into thinking. Our awareness seems to move to the back burner of our mind, allowing us to concentrate and focus using our cognitive mind.

Science has studied these patterns of brain activity for individuals who are doing logical thinking activities and individuals who are meditating. The main point here is that we need to develop our own awareness to successfully navigate between thinking and stilling the mind.

As householders, we are challenged by the cacophony of ringing telephones, honking automobiles, buzzing airplanes, and arguing neighbors. Contrast this to living a monastic lifestyle in a quiet environment that nurtures meditative states. We are not yogis in the mountains, nor nuns living in monasteries where shelter, food, and guidance are given to us. For those of us who are seekers, or looking for personal transformation within relationships, or have a sense of our greater purpose, this is the dilemma we face. We need to know how to find those quiet moments while living in this modern world. The interest in "wellbeing," exercise, supplements, cold plunges, and hiking all echo our need to still our minds in busy times. We need breaks within each day.

In addition, we need the nourishment of peak meditative experiences to give us a taste of what comes with a still mind: peace, joy, touching the larger universe, and personal freedom. We need to sustain these states naturally, outside retreat experiences, within our lives. This is the essential discovery: HOW to identify and sustain these states. Then, we can bring peace and joy into our relationships and our work.

By recalling how peace feels, how joy feels, we do what is called a state change. Just through recollecting, our brain changes from an overly active mind to a quieter, peaceful mind. Science carefully studies these state changes by mapping our brain wave frequency. Eastern traditions carefully map these same state changes by identifying the Bardos.

Bardo States of Consciousness	Brainwave Frequency
Waking Life	Primarily high to medium beta
Dreams	Primarily delta to alpha
Meditation	Primarily alpha to theta
Death	None, yet has awareness
Dharmata	Almost still, yet has awareness
Becoming	Unknown, yet has awareness

Waking Life

This state of consciousness is your daily life—what you are in as you read these words. Many mistakenly believe it is real, solid, and firm. It is the physical world of form filled with social beliefs and values such as material wealth, financial power, and prestige. When we look more deeply into these values and goals, we may find a lack of fulfillment, love, and ultimate meaning regarding our lives. As spiritual beings, we are trapped in a too small container. As we recognize this potential dilemma, we seek the openings that lead to a more full life embracing our potential.

In our usual waking life, we are thinking, pushing ideas through our mind, caught up in repetitious themes of self-talk. This is a state of high beta brainwaves. It leads to stress. Yes, our cognitive mind is necessary for our daily life. We need to be logical. Yet a state of consistent high beta leads to burnout. It is not a problem-solving state.

Early training in biofeedback helps you recognize high beta. There is a monitor screen showing the rise and fall of electrical impulses in the brain. You become aware that you have more than one thought at a time. In fact, you have one thought beginning and it is overlapped with another thought that has not quite ended. In addition, there is a song, maybe even a visual image. You see many waves occurring simultaneously. In early stages of meditation, you can observe this cacophony of activity internally.

It's not about the content of each thought. This is a common pitfall of therapy. Some therapists with their clients get caught up in focusing upon the content of each thought as a way to reduce stress. **You cannot get out of high beta by being in high beta.** In fact, this leads to an endless recycling of old material. The point being that, in daily life, we spend much of our day in high beta.

We can teach ourselves how to quiet the mind by gradually letting go of this cacophony. We need to drop down into an alpha state. Athletes call this "the zone." Walking in nature, breathing the ocean air, smelling the redwoods, and feeling the moisture of gentle fog upon our cheeks—these are the activities that quiet our mind and soothe our soul.

When we are in the zone or in a state of flow, our creativity is expressed. We sculpt, paint, or write in states of flow. Receiving a massage or back rub brings us into the sensuous state of alpha. It is a more meditative state and thus another Bardo. We transition from beta to alpha, moving into a deeper and more peaceful consciousness. We drop down from our head into our senses. We transition from one Bardo state to another.

Psychologically, there are more subtle examples of transitional states. By focusing awareness upon your body, you will feel currents of electrical movement called Qi. The longer you stay focused, the stronger is the pulsation and heat. This is a tool for cultivating energy flow and the stimulation of Kundalini activity (the energy originating at the base of the spine, then running up and through the top of our head).

While guiding a person through a meditative retreat, it is important to lessen their talk and encourage them to focus their awareness on their body. Placing your awareness on the sensations in the body leads to enhanced feelings of tingling, pressure, and heat. These are the movements of Qi through our meridians. Once we can follow our Qi flow, we can direct Qi to our perineum and gradually up our central channel to our crown. This simple practice can move you from a busy mind into a state of expansion.

The changes in brainwaves are only one way to identify the phenomena of transitional states of consciousness. Our direct experience tells us we perceive differently. We perceive our environment differently in terms of sound, light, and space. Our emotions shift from stress, fear, and anger into peaceful, hopeful, and creative.

People doing this kind of contemplative inner work, healing from past traumas or limiting core beliefs and behavior, often report they want deeper connection with others. They seek deeper conversations. When one dives into deeper feelings and expresses that to another person, especially when the person receiving the sharing is also open, a resonance between both people is palpable. We feel deeply heard and understood. Our hearts open in that exchange. We sigh. We physically relax and drop down inside. This is a moment of love. We are at peace and very present.

We change from a more ego based or constricted reality into a more expanded and heart-centered reality. The perceptions are quite different. The interactions lead to different patterns of relating and profound satisfaction.

Now we go further, looking for the space between the thoughts. The space between thoughts exists in a narrow band of theta, just below alpha. One can spend a lifetime looking for and cultivating this portal between thoughts. It is a doorway into many subtle phenomena or the siddhis (powers of meditative masters and practitioners). There is also a wisdom or knowingness that arises as we enter into the theta brainwaves. The cultivation of deep meditation brings us to a state of absorption or Samadhi. Here we can quietly rest in the emptiness of the Void.

From a scientific approach, consider the early work at Stanford using the Faraday cage to observe remote viewing. Psychics were studied to understand how their minds were seeing things that were hundreds of miles away. Later work done at Noetic Institute in Northern California showed adepts in deep meditational states who could heal themselves. Both examples showed that their brain activity was quite low. From an Eastern spiritual approach, this is a demonstration of the cultivation of siddhis that accompany slowing down the mind and dropping into lower brainwaves.

In a single day, and progressively at will, we traverse through waking and sleeping states of consciousness.

Dream Life

There are two distinctly different states of consciousness when we enter a deep delta state: Samadhi and dreams.

Samadhi is a state of deep absorption with no separation of "I" as distinct from "object." The meditator loses sense of time and space, resting in an emptiness of no thought or sensation, often not recognizing they have been gone into the emptiness until they return to their awareness. "Gate gate pāragate pārasaṃgate bodhi svāhā," meaning "gone, gone, gone, beyond to the other shore (Enlightenment, Awakening), amen." Upon returning to self-awareness, there follows a sense of connection and tranquility.

The deep delta dream state is called kunghi-numshi by Vajrayana Buddhists. Here there is no awareness or memory. If we go to bed in a relaxed state, we slide deep into a delta brainwave. Gradually, we move closer to a modicum of occasional awareness wherein there may be archetypal images of vast oceans, heroes, ghosts, or powerful animals. Carl Jung identifies this dream state as the collective unconscious.

The next level of dreams is easier to recall. It is the REM dream state that begins after a few hours of sleep or in the early morning before dawn. These are of a personal nature wherein we are processing daily material, deeper themes, unfinished business, and unresolved situations.

There are many philosophic approaches to dream work such as Freudian, Jungian, Gestalt, art therapy, dance, roleplaying, and journaling. These are more Western. In the Eastern traditions, dream work moves further into expanded states of consciousness, going beyond the personal or archetypal, into the collective. Jung understood this jump and that is why he wrote an introduction to *The Tibetan Book of the Dead.*

As a counterbalance to our cultural tendency to overthink, to rationalize, and to analyze, we need to explore our dreams using non-verbal modalities such as art, music, and dance. Here we find a greater freedom of expression, allowing deeper energetic releases that Jung identifies as our collective unconscious.

**Art Therapy:** In art therapy, we draw or paint the dream. This is not objective art. There is no need to worry about how realistic your drawings appear. Rather, this is subjective, allowing freeform movements, allowing your hand to just dance on the paper. Choose colors that reflect emotions. Art therapy is great for kids and parents alike. Art therapy is most beneficial when you work with a guide who asks you questions about what this squiggle is over here? Or what does this color mean to you?

**Journaling:** Record your dreams each morning in a journal. Even though there may be just a single thread of remembering, somehow the act of sitting and writing pulls back more memory. This is an invitation to yourself to begin remembering. On a deeper level, you are practicing more awareness between different states of consciousness.

**Gestalt Dream Work:** Here, you play out the roles of each person in the dream. This is done using the first person, present tense. This puts the person back into the dream state and you begin to relive the dream. Upon coming to the very last scene, there is an opportunity to continue the dream and even to change the outcome of the entire dream. This is how we finish that which had been haunting us. It is a healing within the dream state.

Now, we enter into more advanced practices of working with awareness in the dream state. There is a direct correlation between expanded states of consciousness in the dream state, our waking life, and in the meditation state.

**The Tibetan Practice of Dream Yoga:** Upon going to bed, begin this practice. In your mind's eye trace the symbol AH (as shown on the next page). The background to this symbol is black, highlighting the outline and white interior. Memorize the symbol. Next, place your awareness in your throat chakra. Visualize the AH in your throat chakra and extend the symbol out into the space of the night sky. You enter the vastness of space upon the trajectory of the AH, which is a symbol of the Void. This is one of the portals into the Void or Shunyata.

Adepts at dream yoga can intentionally both send and receive information to others in their dreams.

Lucid Dreams

These Awakening Dreams are recognized by several qualities. The dreamer is awake inside the dream, aware that they can direct the action of the dream. The visual field within the dream has a pristine quality of clarity. It is more bright and clear than even our waking reality. And lastly, the end of the dream comes in a sudden bolt, and you find yourself sitting upright in your bed. The content of lucid dreams may relate to healing, telepathic communications, or precognition of events.

What is happening here is that the consciousness of the dreamer has evolved through blessings, transmissions, or practice to be able to enter the dream state of another person. One can receive telepathic communications or send them. These are examples of the siddhis or powers that demonstrate an expanded consciousness with some control over awareness.

Dreams are fascinating!

Meditation

While there are boundless practices throughout many cultures, the essence of meditation is to still the mind. A still mind, where there is no thought and no attachment to the occasional thought that arises, allows the mystical aspect of our psyche to flourish. Traveling this path of open exploration invites our innermost nature, our natural mind, to return to Enlightenment as the pure state of our origination.

The key recognition here is that we *return* to a state of expansion. There are many gradations of Enlightenment. We cannot accurately state which level of Enlightenment our natural mind has already achieved. It is merely that we are returning to a state closer to our infancy's purity.

In addition to a still mind, we cultivate a non-verbal awareness. Awareness is neither thought nor any of the five senses. Awareness is omnipresent, unfiltered by ego or self. To identify Awareness, one needs to be still, resting, and present, willing to receive whatever subtle input arises. We may not understand what that Awareness is telling us, yet we can identify Awareness.

In addition to the receptive (or yin) nature of Awareness is its yang counterpart. This yang aspect is focus. Focus is directed without thought and moves with Awareness. To sustain focus is an act of concentration. In turn, this concentration allows us to stay longer or to rest in our experience. It is rather like coming to the frontier of our own discovery on our Path and resting there just a few seconds or minutes longer. Ultimately, we can quietly just remain in these states.

**When we experience mystical states, when we recall our dreams, when we die,
we have Awareness.**

During our waking life as our transformation unfolds, we have Discriminating Awareness that tells us to let go, to not engage in negative emotions, actions, or thoughts. Discriminating Awareness is quick and precise pointing out to us what quality of interaction we choose to pursue. This is meditation in action.

Stages of Tantric Practice

Sometimes in our waking life, we meet people who are extraordinary.

Let me tell you a personal story: When I was very young on this path, I went to meet a newly arrived spiritual teacher. I was led into a small room in the Berkeley hills to sit before an accomplished Tibetan lama. He gestured for me to sit down before him. I sat in silence, totally ignorant of who he was or what was about to occur. I did, however, know how to sit silently, still, gazing directly into the eyes of the person before me.

In our Sufi retreat practices with the Enneagram, we had spent over 30 hours doing eye gazing with every student—a melding of souls. So, I looked into his intense eyes. His years, or perhaps lifetimes, of meditation flowed into me like rivers of wisdom and warmth. He saw deeply into my very soul. It was penetrating. Powerful. Deep. Total. Waves of love energetically filled my very being. He saw me. His unconditional love and total acceptance will be with me forever. This is our potential to be both seen and loved.

Gaze into his eyes. Hold it.

**Dilgo Khyentse, a revered teacher of the Dalai Lama.
Born in Kham, Eastern Tibet, 1910-1991**

Dilgo Khyentse identifies two principal phases of tantric practice: the Development Stage and Completion Stage.

Development Stage

In the Development Stage, you intentionally transmute sights into a form of a saint or deity. Here, you see the Christ-like nature or the Buddha nature in whatever you are looking at—all is becoming its Divine nature. This still requires practice, as we have not yet truly understood how everything we see in an aspect of pure Oneness. You also intentionally transmute sounds into mantras. An example is rolling your rosary beads while chanting Hail Mary. Lastly, you recognize your thoughts transforming them into wisdom.

You visualize yourself and others as divine archetypes. It is seeing the purity within yourself and loved ones. To quote Dilgo Khyentse, "This leads to the discovery of wisdom and compassion...to realize the primordial purity of all phenomena." [2]

For a moment, pause here. Consider the shift of perception that is being presented. In place of judgment of our self, we see the innate purity within us. There is no more self-talk filled with negativity. In its place we turn our mind in a new direction. This is both a psychological and spiritual practice. The Dalai Lama tells Westerners we need self-compassion. The Path of Enlightenment and self-discovery begins with self-compassion.

Once we can settle into self-compassion, we feel an acceptance. We soften and continue to drop our mental and physical tensions. In this deeper settling down into our selves, we leave thinking and simply rest in a peaceful awareness. Perhaps all it takes is just sitting down, taking a break, setting technology aside, sipping on a cup of tea, and feeling the space of a time out. This can happen in your day. It is essential to take these moments.

This progression leads us further into the Development Stage. In the subtle peaceful moment of the time out with a cup of tea, you become keenly aware of your surroundings. You hear more and visually see more clearly. **With the absence of thought, you can identify what we mean by Awareness. It is a sensing of all that is around you.** This expanded sensing connects us with our world. Initially, we connect with our immediate environment. Then, that grows further and we connect with a broader environment, neighborhood, country, and planet. We connect with loved ones in our physical presence and not in our physical presence. Awareness expands until we touch upon a taste of Enlightenment wherein we sense what Dilgo Khyentse expresses in these words, "**The ultimate nature of mind is primordial awareness.**" [3]

Like many pursuits in life, our ability to meditate goes through a progression. The introductory practices made popular in our society are the initial or exoteric teachings. Pay attention to your breath, sit still, focus upon our senses, and chant or pray. These may seem simple and yet when we really pay attention, they are quite subtle and profound.

Pause here for a moment and meditate on these three fundamental and sequential practices:

1) Look to the Space Between the Thoughts

Observe how the inside of your brain is a multilayered tape recording. You may have an image, a song, and several thoughts all occurring at the same time. When one thought seems to stop, another quickly has already begun. There is also the song in the background or a fleeting photograph. To even begin to find the space between the thoughts, we must slow all of this down through relaxing, softening.

2) Move into Relaxation by Dropping Down Out of Your Brain

We exhale though our mouth, several times… progressively, more slowly, and more deeply. We enter our physical body with a modicum of awareness. We soften our muscles. We melt like a stick of butter in the sun, oozing into the space surrounding our physical body. Again, we exhale. Paying attention to any tightness in our body, we intentionally soften that area and exhale through the same area. We may even sigh.

3) Give Yourself Permission to Accept All that is Present in Your Life

"I am here, now." "This is my life." To accept is to allow our essential nature to come to the fore. To accept is to listen and then hear our inner voice. To accept is to become comfortable, relaxed, still, and quiet. This is peace.

In time, these three practices will strengthen our inner core, allowing our essence to flow more freely, exploring expanded states of consciousness. Our meditations deepen. Now we put these four practices together.

Rainbow over our ranch.

4) Sky Gazing Transmission and Vajra Guru Chant

I pass this oral transmission on to you as it was given to me by one of the first Vajrayana teachers to come to this country, Tarthang Tulku, Rinpoche. In Tibetan Buddhist practices, we open to Enlightenment through **hearing.** That is why we start this sequence by listening to a chant. We are invoking the presence of an Enlightened teacher to pass on to you the realization of Enlightenment. There are many Enlightened ones in all traditions in our world.

PREPARE (Read these instructions before you start.)

PHYSICAL POSTURE

 ✧ Find a place in nature, maybe on a hillside, or some other private space where you can see the sky. Sit or lie down on an angle, not flat.

 ✧ Position your body with the rays of the sun to one side of your eyes. It is important to not gaze directly into the sun.

 ✧ Slow down your mind.

 ✧ Deeply soften and relax your body.

 ✧ Exhale through your mouth.

 ✧ Accept and embrace your life.

 ✧ Enter the wonderful state of "just so." All is good in the world. You are comforted and peaceful. You are ready to enter a powerful meditation that can open you into advanced spiritual experiences of visions in the sky—a meandering into the heaven realms.

✧   Partially close your eyes. You will notice the rays of the sun upon your eyelashes. You need to quiet your nervous system to the point that there is no movement upon your eyelashes.

✧   When you are both quiet and deeply relaxed, turn your focus to the sky.

CUT THROUGH THE SKY

Gaze into the spaciousness of the sky. Whenever your eyes grasp upon one spot, then focus your awareness, and cut through to go further into space. It is important that your eyes not grasp. You need to let go. This implies that after you are peaceful, soft, and accepting (a kind of oozy quality), you now gather yourself together (collect) with intention. You are collecting your energy to focus. This focus has a vajra like quality, a sharp sword for cutting through and going further and further into the spaciousness.

LISTEN

Listen to this audio chant of Vajra Guru. It is the frequently chanted invocation of Padmasambhava, who brought ancient teachings from India to Tibet.

Om Ah Hum Vajra Guru Padma Siddhi Hum
Om, sound of Creation, Ah, sound of the Void, Hum, Sound of the Heart,
Vajra Guru, Padma, Born of the Lotus out of the Mud,
Siddhi, the Powers/Abilities,

Hum, Sound of the Heart

LISTEN TO TWO AUDIOS OF SKY GAZING WITH VAJRA GURU CHANT

Instructions

Practice

 # 1 INSTRUCTIONS (5 minutes)
 # 2 PRACTICE: Physical Posture (10 minutes), then chant (3 ½ minutes), then "Cut Through The Sky" (15 minutes)

Practice this sequence for 30 minutes each time. Cumulatively build up to 24 hours of practice over a week or month for full benefit. It is one of the most powerful meditations I have learned.

Body Enlightenment: Meditations for the Transformation of the Physical Body

When we do these practices, there are physical changes in our body as well as our emotions and our mind. Our body conducts more energy, electrical current, and light. We can more our Qi as we dance or play music. We feel energized. Our eyes may shine. There is a sense of physical wellbeing and health, even longevity.

At the same time our emotions begin to demonstrate greater patience, generosity, and kindness to our self and others. We may speak words with greater wisdom and show an understanding about life.

Mentally, there is an air of peacefulness about us, a quietude. We are more accepting. We see life more clearly.

These three levels of transformation are also clues that we have dropped down into our physical body with some authentic changes.

Body	Emotions	Mind
Light	Compassion	Clarity
Increased Energy	Generosity	Joy
Electrical Current	Patience	Peace
Longevity	Wisdom	Acceptance

Physically, we feel our nervous system has greater electrical current. It is as if you had been wired for 110 volts and now you are running 220. These are the physical sensations of energy moving in your meridians (subtle energy channels running in tandem with your circulatory system).

In conjunction with increased electrical current, our more subtle energy body activates. Our energy body is essential to this process of spiritual opening. We feel pulsating, trembling, or pressure in specific locations in our physical body. This is the energy system of our chakra network awakening.

Experiencing the Awakening of Our Chakras and Spiritual Channels

Many members of the MOI community, men and women, are having peak experiences of their chakra network and spiritual channels being activated. Many people are familiar with the chakra system. However, you may be less aware of our spiritual channels that run the length of our trunk, from our perineum to our fontanel. The center channel is the Oma Tube, which is as thin as the lead of a pencil resting just in front of our spine.

We need to learn how to move this energy for our spiritual journey to Enlightenment. We begin at the base and progress up to our crown as is detailed below.

<u>*Our Base Chakra*</u> or perineum is viewed as the foundation of Kundalini energy.

As it awakens, you feel a throbbing pressure. Sexual desire increases. The sexual response evolves to contain both a physical desire for intercourse and a philosophical quality of seeking union, greater connection. We taste bliss while simultaneously feeling the throbbing. In furthering the practices below, what had been the hunger for physical intercourse transforms into a mystical state of sensual connection.

In Greek mythology, Ulysses experienced this as the haunting call from the sirens or goddesses upon the rocks as he was attempting to return home. In our culture, these energies arise in ecstatic dancing and primitive drumbeats.

Kundalini Energy Meditation

Remember the practices of acceptance as we navigate the verboten terrain of pragmatic discussion about our sexuality. Sexual energy is natural. We all have it in varying degrees and unique expressions. It is an instinctive energetic drive. How do we harness this powerful force?
Because this guidebook is not addressing biological reproduction, we will focus upon making friends with this energy for the purpose of spiritual transformation.

In the higher sexual tantric practices, we join together with a loved one, synchronize our breath, gaze into their eyes, and harmonize the running of our Qi while seated in Yab-Yum position and in physical sexual contact. So, to be clear, the development of kundalini energy for the purpose of spiritual transformation includes both physical union and spiritual union. It is not dualistic, rather seamlessly whole.

In Reichian Body therapy, you can build up your sexual energy by lying down on your back on a bed and lifting your hips, followed by dropping your hips back down onto the bed. It is a movement from lifting to dropping, repeatedly lifting and dropping, progressively letting go of tension. Do this with a "ha" sound as you drop down. After perhaps three minutes, you will feel increased sexual energy.

Now sit up, straighten your back, and deeply begin to chant the mantra "HUM." Feel a resonance as you deepen the sound. Focus upon your perineum. Hold your focus there. You become aware of heat or throbbing like a pressure upon your pelvis. Gradually, move the vibration of your voice up your torso. Focus upon this gradual movement occurring just in front of your spine. Visualize red. Invoke heat. Our Kundalini energy will move from your perineum up in front of your spine to the top of your head and possibly out your crown. This is the awakening of the Kundalini that opens our chakra system.

As depicted below, this energy can be activated with the mantra "HUM."

"Kundalini Opening" (from my journal)

<u>*Our Dan Tian*</u> consists of the Lower Dan Tian, perineum, and the Upper Dan Tian. Our Upper Dan is approximately two inches below our navel and two inches inside our belly.

I experience this as a large cauldron containing the fire practices of Tummo (the Tibetan word for inner fire). Where other chakras' positions are precise and smaller, this seems to encompass a hip-to-hip width and navel to perineum area. This is our power center, feeding our immune system and the physical transformation of electrical current needed for Awakening.

Opening the Central Channel: A Yogis' Practice

Breathing practices have been used for healing and transpersonal experiences in many cultures. The popular holotropic breathwork created by Drs. Stanislaus and Christine Grof uses rapid breathing, movements, and music.

Prior to their work, Wilhelm Reich developed his breathwork using 3 counts: inhale into the chest, inhale into the belly, and exhale. Accompanied by physical movements and the hands-on touch of a therapist, the client releases body memories. There is, however, a deeper system within the Reichian approach in that each layer of the body progressively follows the chakra system. In the Reichian work, one begins with the jaw to release body armor, then the throat, chest, belly, and lastly pelvis.

Both Grof's and Reich's approach increases our oxygen intake to stimulate emotional release and touch upon transcendent consciousness. What is significant in Reich's approach is that the pelvis is opened last, allowing the powerful energetic release to pass through the upper part of the body without any holding back or unconscious constriction. The inner energetic pathway has been prepared for this force to move from our perineum to our crown, thus becoming a physical-spiritual technique.

Ancient Hindu and Buddhist yogis focus primarily upon the spiritual realm. A profound and secret practice is Tummo (D'tumo). This breath practice generates inner heat for spiritual transformation. Adepts are tested by their ability to stand naked in ice cold rivers, wet their blanket in the water, place their wet blanket upon their bodies, and dry that blanket using the inner heat generated from this practice.

In the 8th century, Padmasambhava traveled from India to Tibet. The first teaching he gave was the Maha Sukha practice. It is a love song to the Universe. This practice, when accompanied by the breath of fire or Tummo, moves the fire in the belly up to the heart chakra. The purpose is to open your central channel. Here, the nectar from the crown merges with the fire of the belly, resulting in extraordinary experiences of bliss.

While our modern internet capabilities refer to Tummo breathing, you will find only ancient paintings or vague references as to what exactly a practitioner is to do.

Included here are specific instructions handed down to me as oral teachings from Tarthang Tulku Rinpoche that describe in detail each step.

The Practice of Tummo and Maha Sukha

PREPARE (Read these instructions before you start.)

✦ Physical posture: With your back straight, slightly tilted forward, legs open about 2 feet apart. You can be in a chair or on a pillow. Here your legs can be crossed. Be comfortable. Place your hands on your thighs, near the top of your knees. Your fingers are on the inside of your thighs. Your palms are on your thighs. Your elbows are slightly pointing outward, away from your body. This physical position will give you a more centered seat as we do the breathing.

✦ Creating the Ambrosia: Focus on your palate in your mouth. Begin a sucking sound like an infant sucking on their mother's breast. Create some saliva in your mouth and then swallow. Visualize the saliva as the sacred nectar of immortality. It has a creamy cool quality. It is sweet. Swallow this sweetness down to your heart chakra. Do this swallowing visualization 3 times.

✦ Focus on your breath: This is the first breath. Take a long inhalation and push out your abdomen as far as you can. Hold your abdomen out as you hold your breath for at least 2 minutes.

✧ Visualize your abdomen: See a cauldron of fire with hot coals in your perineum and base of your spine. See the flames rising up your belly until they touch your heart chakra.

✧ Rapidly exhale with a loud sound.

✧ Repeat this entire sequence while taking a second breath. Visualize hot, hot fire. Tell yourself, *"heat, heat, fire, fire,"* while holding your breath as long as you can. See the flames touching your heart chakra and meeting with the creamy cool nectar in your heart.

✧ Rapidly exhale with a loud sound.

✧ Repeat this entire sequence taking a third breath. Visualize hot, hot fire shooting flames upwards. Tell yourself, *"heat, heat, fire, fire."* Holding your breath as long as you can! Make a gigantic effort to feel hot and see burning hot coals in your pelvis. This time as the flames reach your heart, there is a sizzling sound. The creamy nectar of ambrosia is co-mingling in a small circle in the center of your heart.

CHANT

Chant: We focus in our heart where the fire and cool sweet ambrosia are mingling. We are invoking the nectar of immortality and infinite bliss. This seed will germinate and grow. We are singing a love song to the Universe, to the heavens. Chant sweetly, singing a lullaby to your newborn baby.

Om Amrita Bindu Java Maha Sukha Soha
Om, sound of Creation, Ambrosia Seed Great Bliss Amen

LISTEN TO TWO AUDIOS OF MAHA SUKHA WITH TUMMO

Instructions

Practice

 # 1 INSTRUCTIONS (5 minutes)
 # 2 PRACTICE (10 minutes)

Our Solar Plexus is located in the front of our body just below where our rib bones separate. It is the home of ego.

For much of our life, our ego tenaciously holds this position in physical constriction. When as children, we have to defend ourselves to survive either physically or emotionally, we maintain this muscular tension in our solar plexus. It is called "body armor." When we are triggered in an emotionally charged and abrasive interaction, we say, "I feel like I just got socked in the gut." What got socked is the ego.

Subsequently, as we begin to open, we become more in touch with this tension. We soften ego's grasp upon our lives. We are less defensive. We come to understand that we do not need to fight or withdraw. We can just let things be and run their course in time. We are making choices to be less reactive. We recognize the distinction between holding onto a grudge from letting go and taking a deep breath. The relief that comes from letting go allows our energy body to flow more freely. We taste equanimity. This progressive softening on all levels of our psyche gives space between our cells that, in turn, allows the opening of our chakra.

Our Heart Chakra is located in the middle of our chest. When fully open, this chakra is akin to a tube running from the front of our body through and out the backside of our body. You can feel winds moving through this tube.

Our heart chakra is essentially, and most importantly, the home of compassion. To fully realize compassion, we need to clear or purify ourselves of the other qualities that also abide in our heart chakra: ancestral karma, personal karma, and current life emotions. **Karma here means only the law of cause and effect. There is no judgment such as good or bad.**

The gradual opening of the heart can take place over years. It is a sensation first of pressure where the muscles have been constricted and now are lengthening, then a sense of aching that is yearning and caring. Yearning still has a grasping of ego, whereas caring is simply compassion and empathy: "I am happy for you."

In the meditation experience below, the person remained in a state of intense focus (Samadhi--concentration) for two hours, asking for emancipation. This meant to "unravel both ancestral pain and physical pain in my ribs (chest) that had been with me for years."

A Meditation Experience: Healing the Heart

"I lay down on a couch to go deeper inwards…to stay in the sacred space along with the other men. I let go and kept surrendering, and before I knew it, deep ancestral and past life pains started flowing. Although it was horrifying and terrifying, I was able to let it fully express through my mind and body. The pain was so strong. I grieved.

I surrendered to the pain and welcomed it with love, with the notion that it's one of my teachers.

I deeply realized how I, and my ancestors, chose these experiences, as Children of God. We chose our pain for the sake of experience, to learn lessons, and to feel the sensations in our bodies and minds. It was so hard and at the same time I had the tools to fully surrender to it and transmute it to light.

I was guiding my pain to the light. I went deep into my heart with my third eye, using immense concentration to find and unwind many knots around it.

For more than two hours, I was unwinding each knot, layer by layer, deep visions of trauma flashed through my mind, and voltages of pain surged through my whole body.

I felt sadness, terror, gratitude, and liberation, all simultaneously. I felt like I was healing deep generational trauma. I felt gratitude to my ancestors, to God, and to myself.

With the knots unwinding, ease came, and blood flow reached new parts of my body—in the back and bottom of my heart, in my lower back, in my neck, in my ribs, and in my armpits. It was spectacular.

Tears went down my cheeks, and joy filled my heart. I was so happy, proud, and grateful while working through the pain. I felt reborn and emancipated. I felt like I healed my heart."

He reports days later, *"There is great relief. Not 100% healed, but close."* [9]

Our Throat Chakra is located near our Adam's apple. It is the gateway to speaking our truth.

When as a child you have been reprimanded for speaking up, interrupting the grown-ups, or speaking out of turn, you learn to become silent. This pattern can be repeated over many years, causing us to withdraw our communication. Literally our throat constricts, our breath becomes shallow, and our feelings are hurt. We learn that our voice does not matter.

You can feel this chakra tighten when tears are trying to come up from our hearts. It takes time to allow our inner feelings and inner voice to be expressed openly and with authenticity. In moments like this, just open your mouth and allow a sound to emerge. Be spontaneous rather than trying to think about what sound you will make. Allow the sound. It may be "ahh" (comfort), "grr" (anger), or "ha!" (a sudden loud staccato release of energy). You might cough to let go of energetic phlegm in your spiritual channels that run parallel to your spine in the core of your physical body.

In healing somatically and emotionally, we discover that our voice is legitimate, is valued, and even appreciated. We discover our voice! We learn how to communicate our inner language, this deeper voice, in a gentle and yet centered manner. We learn to express our feelings with a kindness rather than a pendulum swing from silence to outbursts.

This inner voice evolves into a state of flow wherein we write poetry or are eloquent in our choice of words. This inner voice bursts into the songs of mystics echoing the beauty and awe they perceive in meditative states. This is a flow, a rhythmic movement of energy coming up from our belly, traversing our torso, passing through our heart, and out into the world.

Our Third Eye Chakra is located in the pineal gland. It is the home of inner vision.

There are spontaneous drop-in moments where a visual image appears before you like a photograph or short video clip. It is your intuitive ability being presented to you quickly before the filters of ego can negate this knowingness. We often know what we know. It's just that we may not feel comfortable with our own knowingness and hence we deny or pretend we don't know. **Spontaneous images are to be trusted.** They give us information that is important to incorporate into our daily activities.

Many traditions acknowledge this quality of inner vision, often referred to as the all-seeing eye. Ancient Egyptian culture valued humanity connecting with the Divine. Pyramids were designed to geometrically align with the stars. Tombs were created as burial chambers honoring the dead and assisting them in their next life. Our culture today contains remnants of this honoring: look on the back of your one-dollar bill just above the pyramid—there is an all-seeing eye.

A Meditation Experience: The Siddhi of Inner Vision

Inner vision can occur in different states of consciousness. These are my personal examples of the siddhi of seeing:

Bardo of Becoming:	_I see my soul fly into my mother's belly._
Bardo of Meditation:	_I see a saint fill the sky while doing the Sky Meditation._
Bardo of Waking Life:	_I see a chiropractic adjustment of light reorganizing a patient's entire skeletal structure._
	I see an accident on the freeway before I get there, thus slowing down and avoiding a crash.
Dream State:	_I direct my dreams at age three._
	I see JFK's assassination two months before the event.

Our Crown Chakra is located in the center of the top of our head.

As an infant, this spot (our fontanel) was soft. As adults, the bones of our skull have joined together, and this small indentation is closed. Until we energetically open our crown.

In Hindu literature, the crown is known as the supreme center of contact with God, or the breath behind the breath. Chinese masters sometimes called it the inner breath that motivates the outer breath. In Western terms, the electrical current of our Kundalini energy, both liquid and light in nature, races throughout the body and bursts at the top of the head, connecting us with the universe.

A Meditation Experience: Crown Chakra Opening

"Flows of liquid energy move through my meridians, gathering at the top of my head, opening into a bowl. Ornate baroque petals of deep purple, red, and orange adorn the rim. A horizontal orb of white light rotates like a hula hoop about my hips and pelvis, progressing up and down my body in a dance of fluid light, thick viscous rivers of *white and gold. My crown is a 24-karat golden chalice opening. A mandala of multi-colored petals cascades into my brain. I feel the texture of the infinite sky. Distinctly different Enlightened ones come to say hello. The teachings pour in...*

Our thoughts create our realities.

Our attachments create needless suffering.

Our aspirations must be cultivated." [5]

Heart Enlightenment

Please remember that this journey is not linear. It is unique to you. Experiences may pop up seemingly randomly until a collection of direct personal experiences make it clear to you what is actually happening to you. We create a new tapestry of our lives and our understanding as to the purpose of this life.

So, all the meditative experiences that are shared in this guidebook may occur out of the sequence presented here. Yet, we need to begin somewhere in trying to create this map of consciousness.

Thus far, we have spoken about the awakening of the chakras and its concurrent body enlightenment phenomena. Now, we share a recounting of heart enlightenment phenomena.

A Meditation Experience: Luminous White Light Transforms into Unconditional Love

"I describe my memories as best I can.

I know my experience is the same old story from naked men around newfound fire etching their minds with smeared ash. From families in the jungle weaving their knowledge into the textiles of their lineage. From nomadic and domestic peoples. From ancient to those today who overlap my timeline.

My visions narrated these stories without words, acted out a magnificent drama without characters or curtains. To humanize the experience would be a woeful insult to the magnitude of the adventure. This was beyond the physical body, brimming with insight, learning without being taught. I knew everything and nothing. Because of this I had all I needed to know in my journey.

Energy follows the path of least resistance and I was not afraid. I fell away from my body. Divided as if liquid, like the fission of an amoeba. It felt like death but I knew I wasn't dying. It felt like life but I knew I wasn't quite living. Just a breath of consciousness somewhere in between.

I saw my physical self float away from me as if I'd pushed a toy boat into the horizon of a still lake. I surrendered, adrift into a crimson ocean pulsing with the energy of everything once alive and everything yet to be, rhythmically contracting and undulating within its gentle embrace showing me how to ripple the energy from head to toe in orgasmic waves.

A jolting pop penetrated my right ear. The cradling comfort of ego-death's organic bliss now whirred and gurgled as if a plug was dislodged from a bathtub drain. I felt motion, faster, faster, exponentially faster, a simultaneous push from behind and pull from ahead. The climax of this ride propelled me outward into a most luminous white light—I was born! I felt my physical body again, the warmth of it fresh from eternity's womb, passed to my mother for the first time and felt unconditional love as I had never felt before or since. I saw myself as my mother did; I felt the praises of generations past and present, welcoming my entrance into this world…" [11]

Mind Enlightenment

Ancient teachings seem to suggest that the most powerful enlightenment realization comes with the integration of body, mind, and heart enlightenments. As mere beginners, we can temporarily taste perhaps one of these, and years later perhaps another. What is most reassuring is that these tastes last with you. All you need to do is to remember, to reread your own journal, look at your artwork, revisit the subtle details in your mind, and you will be there again. This becomes your own personal meditation: you got there once, now recreate it again and again.

With open chakras, increased electrical current, and a quieter mind free from self-talk, we are ready to expand into emptiness, Shunyata.

A Meditation Experience: Initial Taste of the Void

"I am, for all intents and purposes, a Western householder. I have an iPhone, a family, and a mortgage. This spiritual path is foreign to me. Raised catholic, with some atheism during my time in academia, I had no sense of any experience beyond this worldly body.

I started a meditation practice, because that's what new-age, successful, driven, entrepreneurs did with the goal of performance enhancement.

I don't remember exactly when it first happened, this remembering of an old self. I tasted the emptiness of the Void. I'd be sitting in stillness, watching the breath, and an experience sets in. I feel my body start to expand. My hands seem miles away from my seat of consciousness, which feels like it is somewhere behind my face. My body feels massive, immense, and substantial. I am a small light, witnessing it. Then panic sets in, fear of the unknown. I open my eyes and snap myself out of it.

The frequency and intensity of these experiences reached a point where I could no longer ignore it. Why is this happening to me? This awakening to past monastic lives in the East. I've been told it can take a lifetime of practice to reach the Void or to have fully conscious out of body experiences where I sit face to face with myself.

Most of these experiences happen from nowhere. Though these experiences are new to me in this life, there is something I am building upon from my past. I'm not fully sure where I have been, so I am focusing on listening, committing to learning, to 'turning up the volume' of my inner voice, and allowing these things to happen.

My practice is to sit in the Void, let go of fear, and be in the experience." [7]

Here, the meditator shares an important point: "let go of fear and be in the experience." Initially, as we practice meditation, our ego will grasp a thought or feeling such as "Aha, I got it!" or express a constriction due to fear. We pull out of the experience. **We need to learn how to rest longer in these experiences.** This implies a profound relaxation and comfort in surrender to exploring new terrain. It also implies an ability to focus without thought and then to rest in deep awareness.

Once you can rest in this experience, you are touching the Completion Stage. Completion as a word implies finality. In fact, the on-going process of Enlightenment may have infinite realizations. Kalu Rinpoche (a revered Tibetan Vajrayana teacher) refers to geometric leaps of increasing awareness and understanding much akin to the leap of familiarity with this universe to conceiving of ten universes. Completion as a word implies a very evolved state of Enlightenment where we sustain the state on a continual basis. We live in the Awakened state of Nirvana, wherein the cycle of transmigration (birth, death, and rebirth) leads to spiritual release or Liberation.

There are other meditative experiences that the people of MOI are briefly touching upon that enter the Completion Stage. Granted they are tastes, yet to be sustained. Here are some of these other portals.

Experiences of Light, Love, and God

One of the wondrous mysteries of how this journey unfolds is that it's always **unique to just you!** It is not linear in what occurs (i.e., first you still your mind, then your third eye opens, and then the light always comes). Rather, there are spontaneous tastes of evolved states of consciousness that can drop in at any point. This is what leads us to do intensive retreats. There is a yearning to explore. These tastes spur us on to a more serious and dedicated practice. **You are discovering your potential.** Peak experiences are pieces of a puzzle. In time, these pieces form an entirely new tapestry of how to live a life and the joys that accompany this understanding.

One could think of peak experiences as breakthroughs, removing the filters of judgment and perceptions coming from conditioned ego. We break through into our essential nature. Specific qualities emerge from our deep essential nature. These qualities are predictable and affirm your journey. They are important milestones telling you that you are doing a good job. **These qualities are spaciousness, clarity, light, love, emptiness, and turbulent powerful energy.**

Below are two experiences demonstrating these breakthroughs, carrying a momentary taste of light and love. People feel amazed at these fresh and liberating breakthroughs. Breakthroughs are far beyond what our usual imagination can contrive. Trust the spontaneous!

A Meditation Experience: Perceiving Shimmering Light

"As I lay in bed listening to music, something extraordinary and unexpected happens. As I raise my arm, something wholly other than my familiar limb rises. Rather, a shimmering, crystalline form of an arm, faceted and jewel-encrusted, lifts ethereally from where the flesh and bone version lay, sparkling in the room's dim light.

I sit up. To my amazement, I see my 'physical' body lying still on the bed, unmoved by my will for it to sit up. Yet, there I am, sitting upright, a crystalline version of myself. My physical form continued to lay supine on the bed. 'What the heck is going on?'

My legs continue to lie, unmoving, on the bed. I intuit this radiant form, this essence rising from me, must be my soul, my spirit—momentarily unshackled from the physical form of my familiar 'body.'

A wave of anxiety quickly washes over me. How can I navigate life in this newfound state? The idea of living in a perpetual state of detachment from my physical self is intriguing and unnerving. Is this the end of my existence as I know it? Or is this a new, unexplored journey? I wonder if this is a normal process of the spiritual path that no one has told me about. A few moments later, I look out through my eyes in the 'normal' fashion. I am left with a sense of awe mixed with confusion. I have had this experience on two separate occasions." [10]

Below are two profound personal accountings of God Realization and Divine Presence. Both of these men experience increased electrical current that moves into perception of light within them.

A Meditation Experience: God Realization

The first person's experience comes during an intensive retreat. He has been diligently pursuing his healing path emotionally and psychologically for many years. This preparation has come to fruition as he is able to let go conceptually and rest for some time in the profundity of his peak experience.

"My body relaxes. I feel very still. It is a wonderful feeling to just sort of give in and release control of my body. I feel this amazing energy in my body. It is coming into my feet, going up my body, and shooting straight out of my head. I feel my consciousness leave my body behind. I have never experienced this before. Am I going to be able to 'go back' to my body and the 'real' world? I decide that if this is it, if I am crossing over to some new place, everything is going to be okay. Maybe even better than ok.

I see this column of light and energy going from the floor to the ceiling. I am suddenly struck with the realization that I am God. Not that I am the only God, but that God is a part of me. We are connected. It is an amazing feeling to realize that God is not 'up' in heaven. It is not me and God. God is a part of me. We are connected. We are all connected. I had this wonderful feeling inside of jubilation.

I could have stayed there forever. I do remember quite clearly the feeling of the energy rushing through my body and the jubilant feeling I experience as I realize that we are all a part of God." [14]

A Meditation Experience: The Presence of the Divine

Here is a recounting of a powerful Enlightenment that lasted for nine days. He is a businessman, not a meditator, nor even on a spiritual journey, per se. Yet his intrinsic essential nature burst forth.

During his individual guided journey he said:

"Love is an energy…fluid energy connected to everything…just flowing with colors…my heart beats to the sound of everyone's beat. Feel the closeness. I am that that you are. No attachments. Just let it flow."

When I saw him only hours later, he shared:

"There was light shooting out of my fingertips, and out of my feet. I was on fire and sweat pouring out. I kept laughing. My body was jerking with energy. Trembling, there was such energy. And light everywhere."

His tears of joy poured down his cheeks and words tumbled freely from his lips. We cried together at the beauty he was sharing. His words were understated compared to the intense light shining from his eyes.

Nine days later, he wrote:

"Well, I'm back to myself, kind of feel like I was given a gift of being in Divine Presence for 9 days. Finding myself going back to work mode, with an awareness and sensitivity I have not experienced before." [13]

Samadhi Absorption

Samadhi is the ability to rest in a deep meditative stillness wherein you enter a state of unshakable absorption. Here, simply sitting still changes from feeling stiffness in the joints to feeling solid, silent, and strong. Unshakable. No desire to move. This concentrated state is the pinnacle of meditative practice. Your essential nature merges with the Oneness. Your awareness encompasses self and object into one and the same. Total connection.

The accomplished Hindu teacher, Patanjali states, "The mind in Samadhi possesses power that a normal mind does not, making it the main tool the Yogi uses to achieve the end goal of yoga—the joining of the individual self with the Universal Absolute." [15]

There is a complete absorption as seen in these Zen Ox Herding images. The person and the Ox disappear. There is no subject or object. There is complete emptiness. The accomplishment of Samadhi is key across traditions.

 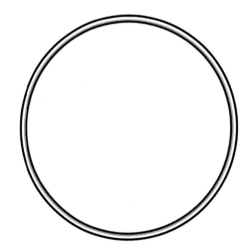

Two Meditation Experiences of Samadhi

Trying to capture the experience of Samadhi is elusive. In the Hindu tradition, there are more than 18 versions of Samadhi progression. There is debate as to, "Is there any awareness in these states if there is no me to be aware?" This becomes the jump into a detailed discussion of what is awareness if there is no thought and if there is no me.

Nonetheless, let us give it a try, a pointing in the direction of attempting to distinguish "no experience" from "experience of no thing."

Here are two accounts of dedicated meditators experiencing Samadhi.

A Meditation Experience: Everything is Presence and Awareness

In the woods of Northern California, there abides a local yogi, a social worker by education. About ten years ago, he left his profession, turning to a life of quietude. He dedicated his life to the path of liberation, immersing himself in deep meditational practices. He shares the fruits of his pursuit.

> *"Initially you may be buffeted by winds of fate and have to master control of concentration, getting closer to directing yourself [in other dimensions]…Then an imperturbable relaxation, unshakable absorption…everything is Presence and Awareness…graspings are dying away as I realize there is nothing to do or become…everything is already it. I have confidence in my liberation."* [16]

A Meditation Experience: Connectedness to Everything

We pause for a moment here while I tell you a story. It is fascinating to see our life events appear to be one thing, and years later discover there was something deeper and more meaningful happening.

This next recounting is from an Air Force pilot who served in the Vietnam War. While on secret missions in Cambodia, a country where politically we denied we were even present, he was led by a guerilla member of the opposing force to a local monastery. They had to cross a river, entering into enemy territory to reach this monastery. Upon arriving, he was greeted by the head abbot who taught him how to meditate. After returning to the U.S., he diligently practiced what was shown to him, ultimately one day realizing, "Ah, this is what he was teaching me!" This is his meditative realization:

> *"My experience [of Samadhi] is there is no ego, no identity, no nothing, no body, emptiness, no thought, no awareness. Until I come out of it. The only awareness I have is remembrance of it after I am out of it. The residual experience after I come out of it is a deep sense of calm and connectedness to everything. I meditate to rid myself of thought, get back to basic nothingness. It's not emptiness. It is a connectedness to everything."* [17]

Putting It All Together

As we leave behind the small teacup of our conditioned ego, as we tame the incessant chatter in our mind, as we familiarize our self with expansion, as we let go into exploring mystical states, as we taste mind enlightenment, body enlightenment, and heart enlightenment, we put it all together into a personal map of self-discovery.

Why? Consider for a moment, if millions of people were to open in this manner, what a different world this would be. We would love our planet and care for her. We would be kind to one another. Our creativity would be boundless. Our personal lives would be filled with clarity and purpose. We would all work together, appreciating differences and commonalities. This is the larger vision.

On a personal level, we begin with baby steps:

✧ Any opportunity in our daily life where we can choose a healthy response rather than a negative anxiety filled response, we are practicing taming our mind.

✧ When we listen to a loved one express their vulnerable voice, we truly are empty and receive them deeply inside our heart.

✧ When we exhale and deeply soften into relaxing, we practice letting go and resting in mystical states of emptiness and light.

These are all preludes to greater events: how to live our daily life and how to die. We are more familiar with the former. Let us dive into the significance of the latter.

Bardo States of Consciousness: Death, Dharmata, and Becoming

These next three bardo states have a thread of awareness that ties them together in a progression over time. Whereas previously discussed, in the other transitional states of consciousness—waking, dreaming, meditation—we move back and forth from one to another. However, in the case of death, dharmata, and becoming, there is a distinct progression. The only exception is that one can flit into dharmata or emptiness in a meditation state, but only temporarily. In the progression we are about to describe, the dharmata experience that follows death, one does not flit in and out. One is in for the ride.

Our deeper essential nature is energy. We have awareness when in our deeper essential nature. It is our essential nature in its most pure form of awareness that undertakes this journey. It is not a reincarnation, as is popularized, because it does not contain our ego or sense of self. Rather, it is awareness.

This awareness travels like a fine thread or filament through our death, our 49 days in the bardo, and ultimately returns to a physical form. This is the case for most of humanity. Again, however, there are exceptions that highly advanced yogis pursue such as the Rainbow Body. Here, the yogi does not enter the bardo of becoming, going beyond any conceptual existence in any conceptual space or time.

For right now, in this human body, we need greater understanding as to how to prepare for this aspect of our total on-going journey—how to approach death and dying.

Death

Like any trip we prepare for, including a vacation, we go through a similar process. Where are we going? How do we wish to travel? We settle our affairs. Then we are ready to leave for awhile. Our physical death is also a leaving for awhile. After going through up to 49 days (sometimes less) of travel in the bardo of death, we are drawn towards a mother and father. We choose our next lifetime, our new destination.

When people do regressive work, they get fleeting images of, "Oh, I have seen this before, sometime a long time ago." These déjà vus can reveal a past life. Today, we have a current life. Tomorrow, and we don't know exactly when, we will have a future life. It is our awareness, without thought, only a sensing, that moves through birth, life, death, and rebirth. Hopefully, we can continue to learn, pick up where we left off, and even meet again with the essential nature of loved ones from the past.

We can change from a sense of fear to an understanding that this is merely a progression, a new chapter. Granted, this approaching journey carries many unknowns. It entails leaving behind what we have known.

If we focus upon letting go, our thoughts and emotions tend towards struggle and sadness. Conversely, once you have been authentic to yourself in your goodbyes, you can focus upon the meditative experiences you have had. This is a crucial focal point.

One by one, recall your expansive memories. Relive them and speak of them to your loved ones. These memories contain information about your approaching bardo journey. Science and medicine have validated there is an awareness even after the body is physically pronounced dead. Near death experiences, as well as those who return to share their experiences, speak of light, sounds, and brilliant colors. These descriptions are similar to your peak experiences when you break through beyond ego. The education you have received through tastes of peak experiences prepares you for the bardo experience of death. So, recall and share out loud the all-encompassing powerful moments of light, the swirling array of colorful energies, the swooshing away of any sense of self, and the sweetness of Divine love. This is your preparation for death.

On a physical level as we are dying, we gradually lose connection to our five senses. There is a loss of life force, of Qi. We withdraw from the environment. We are beginning to travel. To an observer, it may appear the dying person is unconscious or asleep. However, research shows that the person can still hear what is going on in the environment. People describe they are going somewhere peaceful.

As a guide or family member, speak words that support the dying person's spiritual tradition, because we want to affirm their orientation to spirit. It is an inalienable right of our essential nature to exist and be nurtured. What a special opportunity it is to confirm the dying person's understanding of their tradition or uniqueness. This is why we say to a person who is passing, "Go into the light. Go in peace. I love you." These words are reassuring. They help the dying person focus. Our service is simply to support.

We are practicing in this life how to travel with awareness. Any experience you have had helps you feel familiar with the terrain. The more comfortable we are in letting go, in resting in light and expansion, the easier is the journey. Using only our awareness, we need to recognize, "Ah, this is bright light. I know this intense light. I can flow into it."

Dharmata

Internally, this is where the experiences of luminosity begin. Choose a family member or close friend to remind you to focus upon the most brilliant luminosity. This is called the clear light. It is not the brilliant yellow/white light of luminosity. It is the next progression into a clear, colorless, empty, expansive light.

It is not easy to extract a description of the experience of clear light from either realized teachers or written sutras. Because it is such an advanced state of expanded consciousness, there seems to be a hesitation to let the general public know what it is. And yet, it is a human experience available at the moment of death.

"The dying person has the potential to perceive The Clear Light of Ultimate Reality, and recognize it as his own ultimate being. If the soul does this, it merges with the light and no longer has to be reborn. This encounter, however, is quite an overwhelming experience, to put it mildly, and the individual may shrink back from this Light in fear." [19]

In the more advanced yogic meditations of Vajrayana Buddhism, we enter the luminous bardo that commences after the final inner breath. Visions and auditory phenomena occur. In the Dzogchen teachings, these Togal visions spontaneously manifest. Concomitant with these visions is a welling of profound peace and pristine awareness. Meditative practitioners aspire to recognize the clear light appearing at the moment of death *prior* to actually physically passing. Thus, they are familiar with the brilliance, spaciousness, and power of this light.

This precious, powerful, realization of luminosity is available to all sentient beings. Enlightenment.

This moment may be fleeting or lasting, depending upon several factors—your familiarity with this intensity of light, space, vastness, power, emptiness, purity, discriminating awareness, and luminosity. Based upon your preparation and ability to let go, to rest, to surrender in this state of no ego, no body, no thought, no sensation, no reference of familiarity, you can recognize the luminosity and emptiness.

Here, we realize our true primordial state. Home.

The recognition of clear light as the intrinsic nature of everything, or the true nature of all that is, becomes a path to the realization of liberation. This implies the person no longer goes through the process of death and rebirth. This is known as realizing the Rainbow Body.

However, this is also a philosophic choice: to pursue liberation or to return to a physical form. Perhaps this choice hinges upon your sense of service. In both Eastern and Western spiritual epistemologies, there are teachings of the second coming where a highly evolved saint or bodhisattva opts to return to be of service.

"We see and realize the intrinsic awareness of our true enlightened nature of our own mind…realize and maintain [this state] and we attain Buddhahood." [21]

Aldous Huxley in *Doors of Perception* captures the essence of this discussion:

"Would you be able," my wife asked, " to fix your attention on what
The Tibetan Book of the Dead *calls the Clear Light?"*

I was doubtful.

"Would it keep the evil away, if you could hold it?
Or would you not be able to hold it?"
I considered the question for some time.

"Perhaps," I answered at last, "perhaps I could—but only if there were
somebody there to tell me about the Clear Light.

One couldn't do it by oneself.

That's the point, I suppose, of the Tibetan ritual—somebody sitting there all the time
and telling you what's what." [18]

Becoming

After traveling through the Bardo of Death, the next Bardo we enter is Becoming. This Bardo endures until the inner breath commences in the new transmigrating form, as determined by the karmic seeds within the storehouse consciousness known as alaya-vijnana. This is a basic consciousness greater than archetypes and DNA. This is a mind that has all the seeds of human, animal, and plant memory existence that, in turn, pours into billions of cells.

A Meditation Experience Flying into My Mother's Womb

"From personal experience first relived at age 2, I flew through the center span of the Golden Gate Bridge in a rapid and powerful trajectory of light. I went directly into the belly of my very pregnant mother. She was caught in the hatchway of a small sailboat while sailing with my father.

As an adult I did ask my mother if she went sailing on the bay. She laughed and told me a story of getting caught in the hatchway of their boat just before I was born.

Yet, for years I did not put this all together. I did not even speak of this. I had no concept or understanding, until recently, that this was my soul coming into my future body, to be born and raised by my future parents." [25]

Through diligently applying the psychological and spiritual practices in this guidebook, the peak experiences you have tasted will grow and become more a way of life. You discover subtle moments where your ego wants to dominate. Yet with a newfound awareness, you intentionally choose a different, healthier direction. These choices are made in a nanosecond.

Transformation in daily life is a meditation in action. It may not be easy living with one foot in chaotic times in our society, and one foot cultivating "Be, Here, Now." And yet, this is where we have landed. This is the life our souls have chosen to live. The only true stability is to be found living in the present, ultimately living in the Presence. To nurture this quality of love, peace, and connection, find Presence each day, each hour, each breath, each word, each relationship, and each action.

Let's make it simple!

Be
- ✦ Be Here and Now.
- ✦ Be is becoming your deepest nature, your pure mind.
- ✦ Be returns us home.
- ✦ Be is the Oneness.

Here
- ✦ Here means this very space.
- ✦ Here is to feel your body pulsating.
- ✦ Here is to breathe slowly, exhaling through your mouth.
- ✦ Here is to be aware of your environment.
- ✦ Here is to feel the energetic space that appears empty.
- ✦ Here is to be aware of that which is before you.
- ✦ Here is to deeply connect with that which is before you, to literally merge into the consciousness of that person, animal, plant, saint, guru.

Now
- ✦ Now means this very moment, suspended between past and future.
- ✦ Now is the primary portal to expanding our consciousness.
- ✦ Now is the tip of the diving board into the vastness.
- ✦ Now dive.

Live

- ✧ Live in the Here and Now.
- ✧ Live unencumbered by past conditioning and limiting core beliefs.
- ✧ Maintain your empty vessel.
- ✧ Live each moment placing awareness into your five senses.
- ✧ Live quieting your mind through dropping into your heart, reclaiming your body by softening, melting, and deeply relaxing.
- ✧ Live with continual letting go of past-based thinking—the stinking thinking of grudges, conflict, and unresolved issues.
- ✧ Live willing to explore your own potential, the unknown.

A transformation is happening emotionally, as well. Where there has been frustration, now is patience. Rather than engage in quarrels, you breathe and relax, feeling more peaceful. You begin to pause in a busy day and see the beauty of nature in a dewdrop. Your mind eases as you hear the birds call. Rather than force, we surrender. This is the natural process of transformation, as natural as the caterpillar transforming into the butterfly.

People doing this kind of contemplative inner work, healing from past traumas or limiting core beliefs and behavior, often report they want deeper connection with others. There can be a palpable resonance between people when we feel deeply heard and understood. Our hearts are open. This is a moment of profound love.

Here is such an opening between a husband and wife as a result of doing this work.

Husband

"This year marked my 41st journey around the sun…the most reflective and transformative year of my life. My first retreat last December broke me of all the bullshit. …the lies I had to hide behind alcohol.

We attended a concert at the Palace of Fine Arts. Above and Beyond. I wanted to gift my bride of 12 years and mother of two the gift of weightlessness. Before leaving the house, we were in tears with gratitude…going through the house looking at family photos…I held her close during the music and whispered resolutions in her ear: going to bed together every night, playing with our kids, not stressing about work.

We shared the same level of consciousness; she sees what I've achieved…and what I've unlocked.

We got back to fundamentals. US! The co-founders of our family. [We] reconnected stronger than ever. We're unstoppable!

We're all great men. And behind every great man is a more powerful woman. Keep her close!"

Wife

"Every step of my life had to happen just as it did so that we could have the exceptional night together that we experienced.

In my home with my husband looking at photos of our life together, being propelled into a headspace where the love and happiness soar, [we] share beautiful moments of understanding and gratitude.

An extraordinary night unfolds. Whether dancing, grasping hands, or holding each other close, we were one being, reading each other's thoughts and anticipating one another's movements.

The experience elevated all the life lessons and priorities I strive for, allowing for that positive space to be at the top of my mind and on the surface of my heart. The closeness my husband and I shared that evening was unforgettable. We're integrating it into our everyday lives together.

I am very grateful to the MOI community for opening up this space for us. While some refer [to] this as connecting with my husband on a "deeper level," to me we put our love on the pedestal it deserves: knowing we can move forward with renewed vows." [26]

Spiritually, something quite magical is happening. Your Path begins to make sense to you. You come to understand that the difficult times you went through are indeed profound teachings perfectly tailored for your own growth. You are fulfilling the purpose of this life. There is more clarity about the meaning of this life. You are flooded with gratitude. It is palpable, embracing you. You sigh. The weight is lifted. Your mind is at peace. You connect with the interdependency of all that exists. You are Home.

Service

All that you receive, give away.

Pass on your wisdom. Share your heart. Be vulnerable and soft. Be caring.

We are but bubbles of light in the stream of life. Let your light flow to others.

Footnotes

[1] Timothy Leary, Ralph Metzler & Richard Alpert, "The Psychedelic Experience - A manual based on The Book of The Dead, psychedelicfrontier.com/wp-content/uploads/2014/02/The-Psychedelic-Experience-A-Manual-Based-on-the-Tibetan-Book-of-the-Dead.pdf

[2] Collected Works of Dilgo Khyentse, Vol 11, Shambala Publications, London, 2010, pg 296

[3] Works of Dilgo Khyentse, Vol 11, Shambala Publications, London, 2010, pg 320

[4] Works of Dilgo Khyentse, Vol 11, Shambala Publications, London, 2010, pg 311

[5] Personal Meditation Experience of student of expanded consciousness

[6] Collected Works of Dilgo Khyentse, Vol 11, Shambala Publications, London, 2010, pgs. 328, 296

[7] Personal Meditation Experience of student of expanded consciousness

[8] Works of Dilgo Khyentse, Vol 11, Shambala Publications, London, 2010

[9, 10, 11, 12, 13, 14] Personal Meditation Experience of student of expanded consciousness

[15] chopra.com/articles/the-3-levels-of-samadhi

[16, 17] Personal Meditation Experience of student of expanded consciousness

[18] Aldous Huxley, Doors of Perception, pgs. 57-58

[19] Dr. Armstrong, en.wikipedia.org/wiki/Bardo

[20] Joann Bakula, Ph.D. (Transpersonal Psychology), en.wikipedia.org/wiki/Bardo

[21] Madame Blavatsky

[22] Malcolm Smith, "Buddhahood in This Life", en.wikipedia.org/wiki/Bardo

[23] Timothy Leary, Ralph Metzler & Richard Alpert, "The Psychedelic Experience - A manual based on The Tibetan Book of The Dead, psychedelicfrontier.com/wp-content/uploads/2014/02/The-Psychedelic-Experience-A-Manual-Based-on-the-Tibetan-Book-of-the-Dead.pdf

[24] Dr. Evans Wentz, psychedelicfrontier.com/wp-content/uploads/2014/02/The-Psychedelic-Experience-A-Manual-Based-on-the-Tibetan-Book-of-the-Dead.pdf

[25, 26] Personal Meditation Experience of student of expanded consciousness

My Personal Notes for Transformation

Fulfilling Aspirations

As you record your retreat experience, it is important to not edit yourself! Let it flow spontaneously. You can draw or write in prose or poetry. Use colors that move you and express your experiences and feelings.

Limiting Core Beliefs and Their Transformation

To discover and healing a limiting core belief, do this process, slowly, step by step.

- ✦ Remember a scene from your childhood. Look for a "freeze frame" image where this scene is clear to you.
- ✦ Remember what you were told.
- ✦ Tell the person in the scene how you felt about this message. When you have said all that previously was unsaid, now switch roles and become the other person in the scene. Let them say all their previously unsaid feelings and thoughts. Return to being yourself and answer back. Complete this conversation until both sides have said everything. Lastly, note the expression on the face of the person with whom you are speaking. If their expression is softer, more open and listening, even regretful or sad, you are done with this step.
- ✦ Now rewrite the script by telling the person how you wanted this to occur in a more positive vein. Tell them how this changes your current life. Feel this new freedom and strength. Throw off the shackles of constriction. Choose to live in this new way.

Fixation Point	Passion	Virtue
#1 Ego Perfect	Anger	Serenity
#2 Ego Flat	Pride	Humility
#3 Ego Vanity	Lying	Truthfulness
#4 Ego Melon	Envy	Equanimity
#5 Ego Avoidance	Attachment	Detachment
#6 Ego Fear	Fear	Courage
#7 Ego OK	Gluttony	Sobriety
#8 Ego Venge	Lust/Excess	Innocence
#9 Ego Indolence	Indolence	Action

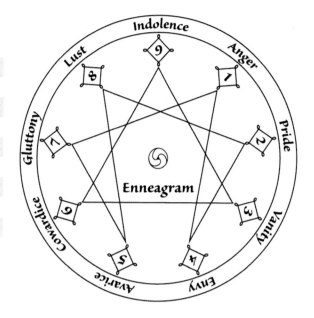

✧ Identify a passion you struggle with daily.
✧ Practice the transformational virtue.

Psychospiritual healing moves through six stages. Each stage is progressively deeper inside you. Identify these stages within you and move through them.

- ✧ Intellectually, we identify an anxiety.
- ✧ Emotionally, we feel stress.
- ✧ Somatically, we feel constriction in a specific part of our body.
- ✧ Energetically, we loosen and pull out the threads or sinews of anguish.
- ✧ Spiritually, we speak to the soul of the other.
- ✧ Lastly, we physically open our eyes to carefully note, "How do I perceive this room right Here and Now?"

What Contemplative Approach Do I Want to Use?

- ❖ Art Therapy
- ❖ Journaling
- ❖ Dream Life (recalling my dreams)
- ❖ Gestalt Dream Work (reliving my dreams)
- ❖ The Tibetan Practice of Dream Yoga using the AH visualization
- ❖ Lucid Dreams

What Meditation Do I Want to Practice?

✦ Look to the space between the thoughts
✦ Relaxing
✦ Accepting (allowing our essential nature to come to the fore)
✦ Sky Gazing
✦ Chanting "Om Ah Hum"
✦ Maha Sukha with Tummo

Made in the USA
Las Vegas, NV
13 March 2024

87125104R00048